Egypt Travel Guide 2023

The Most Updated Pocket Guide to Explore Egypt | Discover the History, Traditions, Culture, Food and Ancient Treasures of the Pharaohs' Land

By
Mike J. Darcey

© **Copyright 2023 - All rights reserved.**

The contents of this book may not be reproduced, duplicated, or transmitted without the author's or publisher's direct written permission.

Under no circumstances will the publisher or author be held liable for any damages, recovery, or financial loss due to the information contained in this book. Neither directly nor indirectly.

Legal Notice:

This book is protected by copyright. This book is for personal use only. You may not modify, distribute, sell, use, quote, or paraphrase any part or content of this book without the author or publisher's permission.

Disclaimer Notice:

Please note that the information contained in this document is for educational and entertainment purposes only. Every effort has been made to present accurate, current, reliable, and complete information. No warranties of any kind are stated or implied. The reader acknowledges that the author is not offering legal, financial, medical, or professional advice. The contents of this book have been taken from various sources. Please consult a licensed professional before attempting any of the techniques described in this book.

By reading this document, the reader agrees that under no circumstances will the author be liable for any direct or indirect loss arising from using the information contained in this document, including but not limited to - errors, omissions, or inaccuracies.

Table of Contents

Introduction 2

Chapter 1: Facts About Egypt 4

Chapter 2: Why You Should Visit Egypt 6

Chapter 3: |The Best Time to Travel to Egypt 14

Chapter 4: Appropriate Clothing For All Seasons 17

Chapter 5: Essentials for Visiting Egypt 19

Chapter 6: Learn Essential Arabic 31

Chapter 7: Itinerary For Egypt Trip 48

Chapter 8: Accommodations in Egypt 55

Chapter 9: Egypt's Hidden Gems 60

Chapter 10: Great pyramid 71

Chapter 11: Top Places To Visit 76

Chapter 12: Best Beaches in Egypt 99

Chapter 13: Local Dishes You Must Try in Egypt 106

Chapter 14: Tips On Currency Exchange 112

Conclusion 118

Introduction

Traveling in 2023 doesn't have to be boring. There are several new travel destinations and experiences that you can enjoy this year or soon with plenty of adventure and excitement. This travel guide will provide you with some helpful tips for the trip.

Egypt is a nation with a rich past and present. The Great Pyramids of Giza and the Sphinx are two of the most well-known ancient structures in the world, and both are located in the northern region of Africa. The Nile River serves as a source of water as well as rich soil for farming as it flows across the country. Visitors to Egypt can take a leisurely boat ride down the Nile or visit the nation's numerous museums and archaeological sites. Egypt has much to offer everyone, whether they are interested in ancient history or contemporary culture.

Egypt is fascinating. the nation has a vibrant past and present. The Great Pyramids of Giza and the Sphinx are two of the most well-known ancient structures in the world, and both are located in the northern region of Africa. As it flows through the country, the Nile River serves as a source of water as well as rich soil for farming. Egypt offers a wide range of events and activities. Numerous museums and archaeological sites, like the Egyptian Museum in Cairo, which is home to over 120,000 artifacts, and the King's Avenue in Luxor, where the pharaohs' tombs are located, are open to visitors.

Anyone interested in ancient history must pay a visit to the Great Pyramids of Giza. These enormous constructions, which date back more than 4,500 years, are considered one of the Seven Wonders of the Ancient World. Another well-liked attraction is the nearby Sphinx, a large statue of a lion with a human head.

Egypt is home to numerous historical sites in addition to a thriving contemporary culture. The nation's capital, Cairo, is a thriving metropolis with an enthralling past and vibrant nightlife. The numerous markets and shops can be explored by tourists, or they can sample some of the savory local cuisines. A boat down the Nile River is an option for those seeking relaxation. Travelers have the opportunity to explore the nation's rural areas as well as some of the smaller towns and villages that are along the river on these excursions.

Overall, Egypt is a place where everyone can find something to do. There is a lot to see and do in this fascinating country, whether you are interested in contemporary culture or ancient history.

Chapter 1: Facts About Egypt

One of the world's ancient civilizations may have originated in Egypt. The ancient Egyptians created a culture that has survived, with its language, government, and way of life.

- ❖ The tombs of the pharaohs were located in the well-known ancient Egyptian ruins. One of the Seven Wonders of the Ancient World is thought to be the Great Pyramids of Giza, which lie nearby Cairo. Egypt's Nile River is the world's longest river and flows through that country. It has been important to the history and development of the country and offers a water supply and good land for farming.
- ❖ The ancient Egyptians erected temples in honor of the different deities they revered. These include the Temple of Karnak in Luxor, which is the most well-known.

- ❖ The ancient Egyptians also created a hieroglyphic writing system, which used symbols and images. Because of the hieroglyphics that can be seen on the walls of temples and tombs, historians now have a greater grasp of how the ancient Egyptians lived.
- ❖ With the majority of its residents practicing Islam, Egypt is a nation with a substantial Muslim population.
- ❖ Egypt's capital is Cairo, one of Africa's biggest cities. It has a long history is well recognized for its congested streets, lively culture, and diverse population.
- ❖ Weaving, pottery, and metalworking were just a few of the skills that the ancient Egyptians were masters of. Their achievements in mathematics and medicine are likewise highly known.
- ❖ Because they believed in the afterlife, the ancient Egyptians preserved the corpse for the afterlife by practicing mummification of the deceased. Numerous museums and archaeological sites across the country house mummified remains.
- ❖ Egypt has a long cultural past, influenced by the Middle East, Africa, and Europe in different ways. These many civilizations influence the country's music, art, and culture.

Chapter 2:
Why You Should Visit Egypt

Egypt is widely recognized for its stunning landscapes and priceless cultural heritage. Egypt is a country that everyone should visit at least once in their lifetime due to its first known civilization's location, the Nile River, two oceans, and unmatched history and heritage. Therefore, the gorgeous nation of Egypt will be your first pick whether you're seeking a location or planning a trip. Listed below are just a few of the many benefits of visiting Egypt:

Egypt is one of the most powerful countries in the world.

Discovering the oldest known instance of human civilization, which took place in Egypt more than 7000 years ago, is one of the great draws of visiting this country. Massive ancient structures like temples, statues, monuments, and buildings, as well as iconic structures like mosques, old churches, castles, and cathedrals, all bear witness to this. The Middle Kingdom, the Old Persian Kingdom, the Ptolemaic Kingdom, the Coptic and Islamic eras, and the Middle and Islamic Kingdoms originated in Egypt.

You will be amazed by Egypt's cities and important sites because of its higher historical diversity. Strong foundations and vocal leaders gave Egyptian culture a reputation for resilience and admiration even from its enemies. Egypt is a fascinating country that will enchant everyone who appreciates history.

Egypt's Astonishing Weather

One of your main priorities when planning a vacation, and Egypt is no different, is the weather. While most visitors from around the world find Egypt to be acceptable and mild, the country does have a hot desert environment. With daytime highs of up to 37°C and chilly evening lows of about 25°C, Egypt's summer season runs from May through September. For almost all wintertime activities and vacations, it is chilly and perfect. There is a 20 to 11-degree Celsius temperature range.

To achieve your goal, February through April and October through November are the ideal periods to travel to Egypt. Sunscreen, sunglasses, a hat, light cotton clothing for the summer, a suitcase or other bulkier clothing for the winter, and if you're going to Egypt, you should bring all the above.

Ridiculous Camel Giza Pyramid

In Egypt, there are a lot of interesting things to do. Here are some excellent behaviors you should avoid.

Fishing, scuba diving, water sports, and horseback riding are among the best pastimes in coastal cities. Cairo is a great place to visit historical sights and meet the locals. To get to the historic site of the regals, you can also ride a camel.

Going on a Nile cruise is a fantastic way to enjoy your time in Egypt. Shopping is a unique activity to enjoy great goods and impressive illusions. Khan el-Khall is Caero's most well-known open market, where you can get anything. You will get the wonderful chance to hike Mount Sinai in Sinai, where you may enjoy the stunning environment and observe the sun rise and set.

The Beauty of the Red Sea Ancient Egyptian Sites

One of the biggest draws for visiting Egypt is the Red Sea, one of the most beautiful waters in the entire world. Egypt, a country that enjoys proximity to the Red Sea, is one of the fortunate countries, and it has several resorts and seaside cities along the shore of the alluring sea. If you're a traveler seeking a short trip, you may pick from a wide selection of upscale hotels that provide excellent services and inviting lodgings.

For those who wish to dig deep and unravel the secrets of the sea, the red sea is the perfect location. Various land activities and aquatic sports are also offered for entertainment. You might have a brilliant idea. Take a trip to the desert areas close to the sea to see Bedouin culture and discover the desert's natural beauty, including its immaculate golden dunes and breathtaking mountains. It would be best if you allotted time when traveling to Egypt to tour the Red Sea resorts and cities.

Numerous significant religious symbols can be found in Egypt.

Why should I travel to Egypt is a question you might ask. Consequently, one of the causes would be the authorized tourist destinations. Visit the stunning ancient religious monuments in Egypt to see a sample of the many different religions and lifestyles Egyptians have long practiced. The Village, Philae, Hatcheptut, Karnak, Abu Simbel, and many other locations still represent the psychedelic era. In addition, Coptic churches and Jewish synagogues such as the Ben Ezra and Hanging Churches are visible.

For more than 14 centuries, Egypt has been an Islamic country, and for many of those centuries, it also functioned as the center of the Islamic kingdom. As a result, it is home to numerous historical monuments, such as those of El Hussein, Amr Ibn Al, Ibn Toulouse, Muhammad Al, and El Azhar.

You will travel along Moses Mount in Egypt, also called Jabal Al Tor, a revered landmark in Snap, northeastern Egypt. Muslims, Christians, and Jews are among the many religions whose adherents visit Mount Moses because it is holy. They contend that Allah gave the Prophet Moses divine instructions at that time. Peace be upon him. Beautiful and perfect for climbing and hiking, the mountain. You will have the opportunity to see a notable sacred place and take in the stunning mountain scenery in this area.

Enjoy Delectable Egyptian Cuisine

Egypt is home to one of the tastiest foods on earth. The cuisine has been inspired by the nations nearby. Egyptian cuisine not only tastes great but also characterizes situations and moods. Egyptians prepare separate meals for happy and sad situations and serve unique food at certain times.

Try some of these delectable foods if you find yourself in Egypt: Ful medames, Ta'meya, Koshari, Fattah, Hawawish, and Shawarma. Along with wonderful Egyptian desserts such as Fitter, Baklava, Barbour, and Kunafa, you may also savor tasty pieces of bread like Eh Balad and Eh Ham. Cheese varieties popular among Egyptians include Mmm, Domat, and Arieeh. Your trip will be even more delicious, thanks to Egyptian cuisine.

Magnificent Historical Attractions in Egypt

Egypt could be home to some incredible historical sites and monuments. You will remember the numerous tunnel lights Egypt has throughout the nation. Alexandria is a seaport city where you may find the Catacombs, the Qatar Tower, and the beautiful Alexandrian Library. The majestic Giza Pyramid Complex is located in Cairo, north of Alexandria. You may visit the Sphinx, the Village Temple, the Sahara Step Pyramid, the Great Three Pyramids, and more. To see the Luxor Temple and the Karnak Complex on the far bank, travel to Luxor in southern Egypt (sometimes called higher Egypt). You can see the Royal Avenue, the Hatshepsut Temple, and the Memorial Column from the best bank.

The ancient city of Aswan is located in the far south, close to the Sudanese border. The Philae Temple, the Unfinished Obelisk, and the Great Thanks to the Land in the Middle of the Nile and other wonders are a land of magic and wonders. The High Dam of Aswan, Egypt's most illustrious achievement of the 20th century, is another location you can visit. Awaan is when one enters the peculiar teachings of Abu Simbel. Due to its abundance of historical sites and landmarks—which might fill entire volumes—Egypt is the perfect vacation spot for travelers who enjoy culture.

Egyptian culture is vibrant

With a rich and fascinating history, Egypt is one of the most renowned countries in the ancient world of civilization. It provides a wide range of cultural experiences and some of the most distinctive landscapes on the planet. Egypt's culture is present throughout the entire nation. Both the majestic metropolis of Cairo, Egypt's capital for centuries, and the lovely seaside city of Alexandria can be found in the country's north.

Upper Egypt is the part of Egypt that is the most impressive to observe. Here, you can go back in time and explore the history of Ancient Egypt in a special way. Visit the famous cultural sites and landmarks by taking a cultural trip from Luxor to Aswan.

To Enjoy a Narrow Cruise Between Luxury and Aspiration

One of the few remaining attractions in Egypt is the Nile River. The beauty of the Nile can be discovered in a variety of ways. One alternative is to take a leisurely Nile cruise and discover the interesting history of Upper Egypt. Along with the Aswan's historical landmarks, you will find the top sights of Luxor City on both sides.

You'll also make stops at the beautiful temples of Kôm Ombo and Edfu on the way from Luxor to Aswan. Numerous lavish Nile cruises with top-notch accommodations, extravagant extras, and top-notch service are available in Egypt. I'll never forget this extraordinary occasion, which I will treasure forever.

Warming and welcoming of Egyptian citizens

The kindness and hospitality of its people is a wonderful additional reason to visit Egypt, or any country in general. Egyptians are highly friendly and compassionate individuals who like supporting anyone who asks for help. Additionally, they are genuinely joyful individuals that enjoy interacting and accepting from strangers.

Like any other nation, Egypt has a diverse variety of social strata, but what distinguishes Egyptians from other people is their affection for one another and desire to provide a helping hand to those in need. They take pleasure in imparting their traditions and rituals to others. To connect with Egyptians and prevent unintentionally offending someone, you should have some grasp of their cultural traditions.

Egypt has the longest Nile River in the world

As a result, the area of Egypt is split into two sides, running from Rasheed and Namaste in the north to Aswan in the south. With a length of more than 6,600 kilometers, the Nile is thought to be the world's longest river. The Mediterranean serves as the destination. North of Egypt is the sea.

Because they thought the eastern bank symbolized life and the western bank represented death and the afterlife, the ancient Egyptians built their tombs and burial sites on the western bank while residing on the eastern bank. The Nile River symbolizes power and majesty in Egyptian culture. A well-known adage in their language declares that Egypt is the Nile's gift.

Chapter 3:
|The Best Time to Travel to Egypt

The best time to visit Egypt depends on a number of variables, including the weather, your trip itinerary, and others. In general, the fall and winter months of October through April are the ideal times to visit Egypt. Due to the milder and cozier weather, these months are ideal for seeing the country's many outdoor attractions. In addition, this is a great time to visit the beaches that line the Red Sea. The best times to visit Egypt's desert regions are during the colder months of the year, when the weather is more suitable for hiking and camping.

The best time to travel to Egypt depends on a number of variables, some of which are:

- **For pleasant weather:** Between October and April, in the fall or winter, is the best time to visit Egypt for beautiful weather. The colder and less humid weather makes these months perfect for travel and outdoor activities.
- **For cultural events:** All throughout the year, Egypt is the site of a number of fairs and cultural events. Two of the most well-known events are the International Film Festivals of Cairo and Luxor. Both occur in corresponding months of November and February. You should plan your travel accordingly if you wish to attend these events.
- **Beach vacations:** The best time to visit Egypt to enjoy the beaches is during the winter, which lasts from December to February. The best time to

unwind and enjoy the scenery is now. Red Sea Shoreline due to the cooler climate and less congested beaches.
- ❖ **For desert excursions:** The milder months of the year, from October to April, are the ideal seasons to visit Egypt for desert adventures. These months are typically dry and sunny with more bearable temperatures for camping and hiking in the desert. The best time to go depends on your vacation plans and the sights and activities you want to undertake in Egypt. Plan ahead and conduct some research on local weather trends, festivals, and other events to make the most of your trip.

Visa Requirements

You could require a visa to enter Egypt depending on where you are from and why you are traveling there.

Most foreign visitors to Egypt will need a visa in order to enter the country. You can visit the country just once and stay there for up to three months with a single-entry visa. On the other hand, a multiple-entry visa allows you to enter and exit the country numerous times over the course of a specific period of time.

To apply for a visa, you must submit an application form, a current passport, two passport-sized photos, and any other required paperwork, like a letter of invitation from a host in Egypt or evidence of travel insurance. You can also be required to pay a visa fee.

The Egyptian embassy or consulate nearest to you should be contacted before making travel arrangements to ensure you have the necessary papers. It's important to remember that some countries have specific visa requirements or agreements with Egypt.

As the security situation in the nation can swiftly change, it's a good idea to study the most recent travel advisories before making travel arrangements to Egypt.

- ❖ Egypt has a few countries with special visa policies or agreements. Here are several examples:
- ❖ In order to enter Egypt and stay there for up to 30 days, people from the United Arab Emirates, Bahrain, Kuwait, Oman, and Qatar are not need to have a visa.
- ❖ Citizens of the European Union, the United States, Canada, and a number of other countries can obtain a single-entry or multiple-entry visa upon arrival in Egypt.
- ❖ Some nationals, including those of Russia, China, and several African and Latin American countries, can apply for a visa at the Egyptian embassy or consulate in their home country before traveling to Egypt.

It is typically advised to get in touch with the Egyptian embassy or consulate nearest to you before making travel plans in order to have the best assurance that you have the required documentation and are aware of any special visa requirements or agreements that may apply to you.

Chapter 4: Appropriate Clothing For All Seasons

Spring (March - May): It's crucial to pack clothing that can be worn in a variety of climates because spring in Egypt can be hot during the day and cool at night. Cotton and linen are excellent options because they are light and breathable. Bring shorts, t-shirts, and walking shoes for activities during the day. When visiting holy locations, it's crucial to dress modestly and cover your knees and shoulders. If you're traveling to the desert or a seaside region in the evening, you might want to bring a light jacket or sweater.

Summer (June - August): Egypt experiences a hot, dry summer with frequent highs above 100°F (38°C). Pack breathable, light clothing that is loose-fitting and made of cotton or linen, such as blouses, skirts, and slacks. Dresses and shirts with short sleeves are perfect for staying cool. To shield oneself from the sun, you should also bring a wide-brimmed hat, sunglasses, and sunscreen. For activities during the day, sandals or airy shoes are ideal. To avoid mosquito bites at night, wear long sleeve shirts and jeans.

Fall (September - November): In Egypt, fall is comparable to spring in that the days are warm and the evenings are cool. Bring skirts, shorts, and t-shirts in addition to lightweight, breathable fabrics like cotton and linen. When visiting holy locations, it's vital to dress conservatively, covering your knees and shoulders. If you're traveling to the desert or a seaside region in the evening, you might want to bring a light jacket or sweater.

Winter (December - February): It's crucial to carry warm clothing for the winter because Egypt's winters can be chilly, especially at night. Since temperatures might change during the day, layering is essential. Bring wool or fleece-made pants, sweaters, and coats that are warm. You can also stay warm by wearing a hat and scarf. Closed-toe shoes may be required on cooler days, but comfortable footwear is still crucial. A waterproof jacket or umbrella should also be packed because Egypt experiences rainy weather in the winter.

Chapter 5:
Essentials for Visiting Egypt

Dress

A largely traditional community with predominating religious traditions, any clothing showing off body parts, such as shorts or sleeveless tops, may be frowned upon. Both men and women can benefit from this. Women should be aware of the need to hide their cleavage and refrain from wearing clothing that is too form-fitting. Maxi dresses or long flowing skirts would be excellent. Also helpful would be a small cardigan or headband to cover shoulders. When entering a mosque, the head must be covered.

Even though local ladies typically wear sandals while they walk, it would be more sensible for tourists to wear comfortable shoes given the unclean streets and rough footpaths. Also acceptable are sandals. When entering an Islamic place of worship, one must take their shoes off.

Money

First of all, due to regular use, money bills are frequently gritty and odorous; hand sanitizer will be helpful here. Second, whenever you go out, always have tiny bills and pennies with you. The custom of giving tips, or "baksheesh," is very common. For any service, whether taxi drivers, bellhops, waiters, people who supply toilet paper in public facilities, or people who assist you with loading or unloading luggage, they will anticipate it.

Tourists are warned that con artists are present. They could be encountered right away after stepping off the plane.

Like other tourist destinations in the Middle East, there are a lot of people who will offer uninvited help or advice for transportation or shopping. Typically, they would offer to take you to a well-known store owned by their cousin or act as your finest guide in exchange for a decent gratuity, or "baksheesh." It would be safer to simply thank them and ignore them. Many of the tours they recommend are pricey. To avoid such traps, traveling in a group is the safer option.

Trains

Giza is the location of the Luxor train station. Ramses station also has a lot of trains departing. There are 3 classes: Local, Express, and Ordinary. Express trains have more space and are more comfortable. Delays frequently occur. Cairo-Alexandria, Cairo-Luxor, and Luxor-Aswan are the main train routes with the highest regularity. Watania runs the trains between Cairo and Luxor and Aswan. Online train reservations are available. The Egyptian railways operate more mainline trains. Direct trains are air-conditioned and include first-class coaches; they are primarily utilized by wealthy Egyptians and tourists. Air Conditioned compartment for two from Cairo to Luxor (313 miles) costs $110, single $80, and travel time is close to 12 hours.

Roads

The major cities are connected by a decent road system. In non-urban locations, the roads may be in poor condition, rutted, or have sections of erosion. The minor roads aren't terrible, although one could encounter loose sand, mud, or gravel on them. The long road journey is in straight portions because of the flat landscape.

When traveling through rural areas, one should always be on the alert for speed bumps that the people have unlawfully placed across the road. These might harm the car's suspension. Police checkpoints can be found driving outside of Cairo and they demand identification like a passport and driver's license.

Buses

People use the trams and buses run by government transportation firms in Cairo for public transportation. Between 05.30 in the morning and 00.00 at night, the services are frequent. Overcrowding, however, is a nuisance, especially during rush hour when finding a place to stand is challenging. Arabic text is used on the front to represent the route and the destination's name. Inside the bus, the kumsari, the conductor, collects the fare. Smoking is prohibited.

There are inter-city services, but there is no direct bus route connecting Cairo with Luxor; the journey takes a long time and is not recommended for tourists. Five companies servicing their respective industries offer long-distance services. The Canal area, Mansurah, and Damietta are served by the Eastern Delta; Kafr al-Shaykh and Manufiyyah, Tanta, by the Middle Delta; Damanhur, Alexandria, by the Western Delta; and the Sinai regions are served by the Sinai Bus Company. These businesses have offices in Cairo.

Three different bus service kinds exist. First, those who call at every intercity station with fewer stops. A dedicated seat, a cleaner bathroom, and food are all included in the express class, which provides superior comfort. Air conditioning is only available in the deluxe class; other classes play with open windows, which can allow in a lot of dust.

Taxis

These are in the major cities and are hailed by calling "taksi" with a raised hand. The front of the dashboard houses the fare meter, which operates at the government-approved rate. The authorized fare is also valid for travel outside of Cairo. The government-owned corporation also runs a 24-hour limousine "Misr" service throughout the city.

Car Rentals

These can be rented through the hotel or travel agencies; the cost varies by vehicle type. A foreign driving permit is good for six months.

Carriages

Taking a carriage is a lovely way to see rural areas and provincial cities. Their ranks are typically found close to the station, and their drivers frequently have a better understanding of the neighborhood than taxi drivers. Although slower, they can frequently go places that a taxi cannot.

Airport to City

While many others operate on fixed routes and tariffs, the standard white and yellow taxis have fare meters. It is generally preferable to determine the reasonable rate for a cab ride from the hotel and establish the fare before boarding. In Cairo, a 3-km cab ride may cost between EP 2.50 and 3.00. Shuttle services between the airport and the city are available for between EP

25 and 100; for "limousine services," which are similar to taxis but have set costs depending on your location and desired level of comfort, between EP 65 and 470 are available. The fixed fare for the public bus service from the airport to the city center is 70 Piaster. At Piasters 20–50, the metro travel within the city is the most affordable.

A few years ago, Uber services were introduced in Cairo and Alexandria. These have gained popularity and will probably spread to other cities. There are more than 90,000 Uber drivers in Cairo alone.

Security and Law and Order

Despite rumors of terrorism in its neighbors, Egypt has long experienced a state of relative calm and stability. There have been terrorist attacks in the past that targeted tourists; the most notable ones are the 1993 explosion on a tour bus at the Giza Pyramids, the 1993 assassination of American and French tourists in Cairo, the 1997 massacre in Luxor that left 62 tourists dead, the 2004 bombing of a French flight carrying French tourists out of Sharm El-Sheikh, and the 2004 bombings at tourist hotels in Sinai. Even if the government has put in place security measures, travellers still need to use common sense safety precautions like staying indoors at night in unfamiliar areas, particularly in the desert. Travel to North Sinai is not advised, and only necessary travel to South Sinai is advised, according to American and British travel advisories. Safer places to visit include Sharm El Sheikh.

In addition to terrorist attacks, Egypt has since 2011 faced substantial political unrest that has had an impact on the internal situation. This has occasionally entailed violent protests and disruptions that have claimed many lives.

There have recently been protests, marches, and demonstrations all around Egypt. If you become aware of any rallies, marches, or demonstrations nearby, you should leave the area right once because the situation may alter abruptly and without warning. For crowd control, police have historically employed water cannons, tear gas, birdshot, and live bullets.

Foreigners who participate in any political action or activities that are critical of the government run the danger of being detained.

Road accidents are frequent as a result of bad driving habits, infractions of the traffic laws, and poor road conditions. Avoiding nighttime driving is safer, especially outside of major cities and tourist destinations. Make sure your insurance is sufficient.

If you plan to travel off-road, hire a knowledgeable guide and secure the necessary permits from the Ministry of the Interior. For foreigners traveling from Nuweiba south to Abu Ghaloum and east to the Coloured Canyon, as well as evidently for other particular places of Egypt, a tourist police permission is required.

Egypt has a typically low crime rate, however over the years, travelers have occasionally been victims of armed robberies, muggeries (including in taxis), sexual assaults, and break-ins to lodging and vehicles. Pickpockets and bag snatchers should also be avoided.

Tourism Companies

Intrepid: (https://www.intrepridtravel.com) It runs excursions lasting one to two weeks. The two-week journey costs $1300 and travels through most of the nation by bus, boat, and train. Additionally, it offers vacation packages for nearby nations like Jordan, Palestine, and Israel.

Memphis Tours: (https://www.memphistours.com) Various packages are available from an old firm, ranging from camel rides from Sharm el-Sheikh to full or half-day tours of Cairo or Alexandria ($35–$90 per person). Additionally, they provide Nile cruises, Lake Nasser, and Luxor-Aswan trips along the Nile (from $500 per person for a 4-day vacation). Additionally, they plan trip packages for groups to see the major Cairo and Luxor attractions. Depending on the activity, the price per person starts at $1100.

Look at Egypt Tours:

(https://www.lookategypttours.com) It offers a range of day trips to places like Cairo, Alexandria, Luxor, and Sharm el-Sheikh, with prices ranging between $50 and $150 depending on the number of passengers. With meals, guides, and transportation, longer tours lasting eight to ten days may cost $1500-$2000. People who are interested in the nation's prehistoric past frequently take specialized vacations like two-week archaeological expeditions.

On the Go Tours:

(https://www.onthegotours.com) It provides travel within Egypt and to a number of its neighbors. Another reputable travel agency. Its eight-day Cairo to Luxor journey is reasonably priced at $400 and includes visits to the Valley of the Kings, the Pyramids of Giza, the Egyptian Museum in Cairo, the temples in Luxor, and the Egyptian Museum in Cairo. Backpackers should consider using it because it arranges affordable accommodation.

Jakada Tours: (https://jakadatoursegypt.com) It offers tours ranging between a week and ten days for $600–$1000 through a relatively smaller agency. It boasts a pool of skilled tour operators.

Exodus Travels: (https://exodustravels.com) offers a nine-day Nile cruise from Luxor that, for a party of 20 travelers, strikes an excellent balance between quality and cost (around $1,400 per head, all-inclusive). Including other tour companies, it also offers a lengthier trip lasting two weeks that visits important locations like Alexandria and the Valley of the Kings. The cost per person starts at $ 2000.

Beyond the Nile Tours:

(https://beyondtheniletours.com) With a flexible range of activities, such as a balloon flight over the Pyramids ($100) and other optional outings, it offers three tours that last between eight and fifteen days. The lengthy excursions start in Cairo and include flights to Luxor and a Nile cruise that take visitors to the Valley of the Kings and other locations. Another choice is to unwind at a resort on the Red Sea. Depending on the activity, costs per person range from $ 1200 to $ 1400.

Continental Tours:

(https://www.continentaltours.com) It has been in business for 30 years and has built up a sizable network of domestic and foreign travel agents.

Located in Garden City at 7 Latin America Street, Isis Building, next to the US Embassy.

Budget Hotels

The price for a double room, which may vary depending on the season, is typically displayed by hotels.

To find the widest selection of hostel accommodations, go to Hostelworld. Booking.com is used by frugal travelers to compare hotel and guesthouse rates.

Even if it might not be difficult to find a hotel without a reservation, it will be more practical to do so for the first night.

For free or if the stay is longer than two nights, several hotels offer airport pickup.

There's a chance that cribs for more babies won't fit in the room.

For less than $20 per night, the cheap hostels provide basic amenities, some of which are shared. These include Wake Up Cairo, Freedom Hostel, Dahab Hostel, Cecilia Hostel, One Season, and King Tut Hostel in Cairo.

Cairo

The Best View Pyramids Hotel is located in the Al Haram neighborhood of Giza, 1050 meters from the Giza Pyramid, at 13 Gamal Abd Nasser Street. It costs $50 with breakfast.

1.2 kilometers from the Giza Pyramids and 40 minutes' drive from the airport are the Pyramids Village Inn (Dr. Eglal Mohamed St., Cairo), which costs $45 with breakfast.

Al-Azhar Park may be reached by foot in 25 minutes from the Atlas International Hotel, which is situated at 2 Mohamed Roushdi St. $37

Near the Dokki metro station, the Pyramids Eyes Hotel is $57 including breakfast.

The Pearl Hotel in Maadi offers 48 rooms with sea views for $69 with breakfast and is situated close to The District Mall at 32 Road 7 and Road 82.

A golf course is available at the Central Paris Hostel, 5 Talaat Harb St, for $62 including breakfast.

28 Gamal Abd El Nasir Nazlet Alsman, Giza District, close to the Meidum Pyramid, Maskadi Pyramids View, $28.

14 Abou Al Hool Al Seiaji Pyramids Plateau is the 3-star Great Pyramid Inn in the Giza region; breakfast is $68.

Two-star Milano Hotel in the Dokki neighborhood, $43 with breakfast, a short distance from Nasser subterranean station.

34 Talaat Harb St., Miami Cairo Hostel, $24, is close to the Egyptian Museum.

The Grand Palace Hotel is 1.7 kilometers from the Islamic Art Museum and costs $37.

Cairo, Giza Pyramids Inn, 6 Sphinx St, Pyramids Giza, Sufi Pyramids Inn, 19 Abou Al Hool Al Seiahi St, $ 39 $61 including breakfast.

Nour Hostel is located in the Dokki neighborhood at 34 Talaat Hzab St., 20 minutes by foot from Cairo Tower. including breakfast, $27.

Near Tahrir Square, in the Dokki neighborhood, lies the New City Hotel, located at 5 Taalat Harb Street. Near Cairo Ramses Station, at the 66 El Gomhoria Street Victoria Hotel, for $34, $36.

Liberation Square is beside Tahrir Plaza, which is located at 19 Meret Basha St. $57.

Gamal Abfd El Abd El Nasr St., Sunshine Pyramids View Hotel, Nazlet El Semman, $27.

6 Gerier St., Nazlet El Semman, Giza, Marvel Stone Hotel $61 including breakfast.

Downtown Cairo's Abdeen Palace Hotel is located at 2 Sabry Abo Alam St. Cairo Paradise Hotel, 41 Sherif Street, Al Fawalah, Abdeen, $35 (tel:20-2-23964220) $15 to $20. Bab Al Louq, Abdeen, and Cairo Moon at 28 Adly Street (tel:20-2-23905119) Cairo Inn, 6 Talaat Harb Square, downtown Cairo (phone: +20-100-077-3210), is priced at $20. 24. Cairo View, 44 A Talaat Harb St, Downtown Cairo (phone: +20 100 801 64426), $20.

Alexandria

Al Mesallah Sharq, Al Attarin, El-Gaish Rd., Semirames Hotel (tel: 20-3-48468370) $20. Alexandria Governorate, Green Plaza Inn (tel: 20-3-3830284) $35-40.

Located next to the Greek Church at 5 Oskofia St., the Alexander the Great Hotel $30.

Cleopatra, Alexandria: 159 Cornish Road, Royal Crown Hotel $25.

Geish Road 133, Alexandria, Kaoud Sporting Hotel (Families Only), $10.

Luxor: $15–20 (3 star) Cleopatra Hotel, Gezirat West Bank, Al Bairat (tel: 20-100-386 8345) http://www.cleopatrahotelluxor.com

11 minutes from the Luxor Temple, Grand Hotel costs $10–15. (tel: 20-100-496-1848).

Khaled Ibn El Waleed Street, Ibrotel Luxor, $40 (4 stars).

Khaled Ibn El Walid St. Gaddis Hotel, $25; 2 stars; Khaled Ibn El Walid St. Mercure Luxor Karnak, $38–45; 4 stars; depending on room; breakfast included; 3 kilometers from the open-air museum.

$35 to $40 at New Memnon Hotel; website: newmemnonhotel.com

Colossi of Memnon, Luxor West, Gold Ibis Hotel, $20 (3 stars) (tel: 20-95-2060984)

Between the Luxor Temple and the Karnak Temple is the $20 3-star Rezeiky Hotel & Camp.

Three-star Pyramids of Luxor, $15-20, West Bank, Gezira Ramla Nile St.

Chapter 6: Learn Essential Arabic

Greetings

No matter if we are interacting with people we already know or those we are meeting for the first time, we always start by greeting them. That is why it is so important to understand how to greet people in the target language.

An instrument of communication is a language. Therefore, in order to interact with others effectively, we need to grasp the fundamentals of having a polite conversation from introduction to farewell.

The following general salutations are suitable for all potential occasions:

	English	**Arabic**	**Transliteration**
Greeting	Hello	مَرحبا	mar'ha'ban
Response	Hey	أَهلا	ahlan

Other phrases that you can use as greetings may include:

	English	**Arabic**	**Transliteration**

Greeting	Welcome to our home/country!	مرحباً في بك بلدنا	mar'ha'ban beka fe bala'de'na
Response	Thank you!	شكراً لك	shokran lak
	Welcome home! (At person's house)	مرحباً في بك منزلنا	mar'ha'ban beka fe man'zele'na
	Welcome, have a seat!	أهلاً تفضل بالجلوس	ahlan, ta'fa'dal bel'joloso
	Thank you! /Thank you very much!	شكراً	shokran
	Goodbye!	مع السلامة	ma'a al'salama
Response	Goodbye! See you later!	مع السلامة،	ma'a al'salama

		نراك لاحقاً	naraka lahe'qan
	Good morning!	صباح الخير	sabah al'khair
	Good evening	مساء الخير	masaa' al'khair
	Good day	نهارك سعيد	naharak Sa'eed
	How are you?	كيف حالك؟	kaif halok?
	I am good	أنا بخير	ana bikhayr
	How is everything?	كيف الأحوال؟	kaif Al'ahwal?
	What's up?	ماذا الجديد؟	mal jadeed
	Long time, no see	وقت مر طويل	mar'ra waqt taweel
	Excuse me	عذراً	Ozran

	Hello, my name is...	مَرحبا، اسمي...	marhaban, ismi...
	See you later	أراك لاحقًا	araka laheqan
	See you tomorrow	أراك غدًا	araka ghadan
	Let us meet again	لِنلتق مجددًا	le'naltaqi mogadadan
	Have a good day	يوما سعيدًا	yawman sa'eedan
	Have a good night	ًليلة سعيدة	laylatan sa'eedatan
	Sleep well	نومًا هنيئًا	nawman ha'ne'an
	How is your day?	كيف يسير يومك؟	kaif yaseer yawmok?
	What's new?	ما الجديد؟	ma al'gadeed?

	How is life?	كيف تسير الحياة معك؟	kaif taseer al'haya ma'ak?
	Nice to see you	سُررت برؤيتك	So'rer'to be'ro'yatek
	Nice to meet you	سُررت بلقائك	So'rer'to be'leqa'ek
	How have you been?	كيف كان حالك؟	kaif kan halok?
	Hello everyone!	مرحباً بالجميع!	marhaban Jamee'an
	How are you feeling?	كيف تشعر؟	kaif tash'or?

Introducing yourself

Making an introduction is crucial. It can, however, be used in place of a greeting. Whether you want to give the person you're speaking to more information about yourself or not will make a difference.

You should keep critical information to yourself; that much is obvious. However, it is strongly advised that you have the ability to convey to others how serious your situation is.

There are naturally two ways to introduce yourself: formally and informally, depending on the circumstance. Sometimes, though not often, greetings are included with introductions as a sign of friendliness, to break the ice and encourage participation in your speech, or both.

Nevertheless, the simpler, the better. In a sense, the main greeting to be used with self-introductions would be *"marhaban"* meaning "hello."

English	Arabic	Transliteration
My name is…	...أنا اسمي	ana ismi
What is your name?	ما اسمك؟	ma is'mok?
I am from America	أنا من أمريكا	ana men amreica
I am a student	أنا طالب	ana taleb
Where are you from?	من أي بلدٍ أنت؟	men ayee baladen ant?

| Pleased to meet you | سررت بلقائك | so'rer'to be'leka'ek |
| I work for... | أعمل أنا لصالح... | ana a'mal le'saleh... |

After our self-introduction, we may occasionally be questioned on a few crucial points pertaining to our interpersonal communication skills. Here is a collection of phrases that are frequently used in certain circumstances:

English	**Arabic**	**Transliteration**
Do you speak Arabic?	هل تتحدث اللغة العربية؟	hal ta'ta'hadath al'arabiya?
Just a little bit!	أتحدثها قَليلا	ata'hada'tho'ha qa'lilan
No! I don't speak Arabic. I speak English.	لا، لا أتحدث العربية. أنا أتحدث الإنجليزية	aa, la ata'hadath al'arabiya. Ana ata'hadath al engli'zi'ya
What is your name?	ما اسمك؟	ma is'mok?

My name is Adam.	آدم اسمي	ismi adam
Where are you from?	أنت أين من؟	men ayn ant?
I am from the United States of America.	أمريكا من أنا	ana men amrica
When did you arrive here?	هنا إلى وصلت متى؟	mata wasalta ela hona?
I arrived here about two weeks ago.	حوالي منذُ وصلت أسبوعين	Wasalatu mondhu hawalay osobu'ayn
What do you do for a living?	تعمل ماذا؟	maza ta'mal?
Are you here on business or on a visit?	أجل من هنا أنت هل للسياحة أم العمل؟	hal anta hone men agl al'amal am ll'seyaha?

I am just visiting.	أنا هنا في زيارة وحسب	ana hona fe zi'yara wa'hasb
I live here.	أنا أعيش هنا	ana a'esh hone
How many years have you lived here?	منذ متى تعيش هنا؟	monz mata ta'esh hona?
I have lived here for six years.	ستة منذ هنا أعيش أعوام	a'eesh hona mondhu sittaty aa'wam
I'm pleased to know you.	أنا مسرور بمعرفتك	ana masrooron be'ma'refa'tek
I'm pleased to meet you.	أنا مسرور بلقائك	ana masrooron be'leqa'ek
We will meet later.	سنلتقي لاحقًا	sanaltaki laheqan

Vocabulary for Directions

The most critical vocabulary to master is that used in directions. simply because it is likely that you want to ask for or travel to a specific spot. They are straightforward and really simple to master as well.

English	Arabic	Transliteration
Right	يمين	ya'meen
Left	يسار	ya'sar
Turn	انعطف	in'aa'tef
Cross the street	اعبر الطريق	o'bor al'tareq
Continue down	استمر في السير	ista'mer fel'sair
Go straight ahead	اذهب مباشرة	izhab mo'ba'shara'tan
Follow this road	اتبع هذا الطريق	it'ba haza al'tareq
Crossroad/Junction	تقاطع طُرق	taqat'oo toroq

Numbers

In Arabic, it is very easy to count from 0 to 10. Like most languages, numbers from 0 to 10 are presented by a single word each.

English	Arabic	Transliteration
0	صِفر	sefr
1	واحد	wahed
2	اثنان	ith'nan
3	ثلاثة	tha'la'tha
4	أربعة	ar'ba'aa
5	خمسة	khamsa
6	ستة	set'ta
7	سبعة	sa'baa
8	ثمانية	tha'ma'neya
9	تسعة	tes'aa

English	Arabic	Transliteration
10	عشرة	ash'ra

Note that all /th/ sounds in the numbers' transliterations are pronounced as those in the word "thank" not like those in the word "this."

English	Arabic	Transliteration
20	عشرون	ish'ron
30	ثلاثون	tha'la'thon
40	أربعون	ar'ba'oon
50	خمسون	khamson
60	ستون	set'ton
70	سبعون	sa'bon
80	ثمانون	tha'ma'non
90	تسعون	tes'on
100	مائة	ma'aa
1000	ألف	a'lf

10000	آلاف عشرة	ashart alaf
100,000 (One hundred thousand)	ألف مائة	meet alf
1,000,000 (One million)	مليون	million
10,000,000 (Ten million)	ملايين عشرة	ashrat malayeen
100,000,000 (One hundred million)	مليون مائة	meet malyoon
1,000,000,000 (One billion)	مليار	mil'yar

To get combined numbers, there are fixed rules to follow:

Numbers from 11 to 19

We simply place the number we want +10 (Ashar) as follows:

English	Arabic	Transliteration
11	أحد عشر/إحدى عشر	ahada ashar
12	اثنا عشر	ithna ashar
13	ثلاثة عشر	thalathata ashar
14	أربعة عشر	arb'aata ashar
15	خمسة عشر	kham'sata ashar
16	ستة عشر	set'tata ashar
17	سبعة عشر	sab'aata ashar
18	ثمانية عشر	thamanyata ashar
19	تسعة عشر	tes'aata ashar

Numbers up to 99

To get combined numbers up to 99, all you need is to add numbers from the first table to numbers from the second table using the letters and sound **"wa"** which means "and."

For example, to say "ninety-nine" in Arabic, you say nine and ninety or ***"tes'as wa tes'on."***

Here's a list with more examples:

English	Arabic	Transliteration
21	واحد وعشرون	wahed **wa** Ish'ron
32	اثنان وثلاثون	ithnan **wa** Tha'la'thon
44	أربعة وأربعون	arba'a **wa** Ar'ba'oon
56	ستة وخمسون	set'ta **wa** Khamson
66	ستة وستون	set'ta **wa** Set'ton
76	ستة وسبعون	set'ta **wa** Sa'bon
83	ثلاثة وثمانون	thalatha **wa** Tha'ma'non
95	خمسة وتسعون	khamsa **wa** Tes'on
78	ثمانية وسبعون	thama'nya **wa** sa'bon

The number one hundred and its multiples

The numbers 100 and 200 are the only exception to this rule as they have fixed names regardless of the rule. 100 is known as ***"ma'ah,"*** and 200 is ***"ma'a'tain."*** Other multiples are formed by adding the first number from the first table, and then the word ***"ma'ah"*** as follows:

English	Arabic	Transliteration
300	ثلاثمائة	thalath **ma'ah**
400	أربعمائة	arb'aa **ma'ah**
500	خمسمائة	kham'sa **ma'ah**
600	ستمائة	set'ta **ma'ah**
700	سبعمائة	sab'aa **ma'ah**
800	ثمانمائة	thamani **ma'ah**
900	تسعمائة	tes'o **ma'ah**

The same can be said about the number 1000 and its multiples. The numbers 1000 and 2000 are the only exception to this rule as they have fixed names regardless of the rule.

1000 is known as ***"alf,"*** and 200 is ***"alfain."*** Other multiples are formed by adding the first number from the first table and then the word ***"alaf"*** as follows:

English	Arabic	Transliteration
3000	آلاف ثلاثة	thalathat *alaf*
4000	آلاف أربعة	arb'aat *alaf*
5000	آلاف خمسة	kham'sat *alaf*
6000	آلاف ستة	set'tat *alaf*
7000	آلاف سبعة	sab'aat *alaf*
8000	آلاف ثمانية	thamaniat *alaf*
9000	آلاف تسعة	tes'at *alaf*

By doing the exact opposite of what was done in the preceding instance, number combinations that include 100 and its multiples can be created. In this instance, the hundred or any of its multiples will come before any other number. Next, we'll add more numbers. For example, to say 113, we combine one hundred and then 13 using the letters and sound *"wa"* which means "and." Therefore, 113 in Arabic would be "100+13" or *"ma'ah wa thalathat ashar."*

And to say 1011 would be 1000+11 or *"alf wa ahad ashar."*

Chapter 7:
Itinerary For Egypt Trip

5-Day Trip

A 5-day trip to Egypt can allow tourists to experience a wide variety of sights, with plenty of time to explore and take pictures. This itinerary starts in Cairo on the west side of the Nile, and it takes in towns such as Luxor, Aswan, Abu Simbel and finally Khartoum. It is an easy trip that allows everyone to travel independently.

Day 1

The first day of this trip takes travellers from Cairo to Luxor and Aswan. Luxor is home to the largest temple in Egypt, as well as several other ruins. After arriving in the afternoon, give yourself some time to explore before heading out to dinner. The famous Temple of Karnak is located in this town and is one of Egypt's many noteworthy sites. Aswan is mostly a modern city, and it has excellent views over the Nile that can be enjoyed by tourists who have a free evening after exploring the temple there.

Day 2

After breakfast on the second day, spend some time exploring the surrounding countryside. One of the most famous sites in this area is Karnak, which contains many amazing hieroglyphs. The city of Luxor has a large temple that was built in the Ptolemaic Period and is home to other historical structures. The city of Aswan is also known for its temples, which are called obelisks. These are one of the most famous monuments in Egypt. They were erected as a tribute to the sun god and were used as open air altars.

Day 3

On the morning of the third day, take a boat ride down the Nile, which is a great way to see sites along the river. The boat will travel to the Temple of Philae, which was built when Egypt was part of ancient Nubia. The settlement of Philae was once a thriving city that was abandoned when the Egyptians moved to Aswan. The temple is also home to an altar dedicated to Isis. This is a beautiful building that contains several large columns and steps. Take pictures of this site and the surrounding area, which is known as the Valley of the Kings

Day 4

The fourth day of this trip takes travellers to Abu Simbel, which is famous for its Temple of Ramses II. This structure was built in the 20th century B.C. when Egypt was a new country, and it is considered to be one of the Seven Wonders of the Ancient World. The statues of Ramses in this temple symbolize both strength and beauty. After seeing this site, travel to Aswan for lunch there and then spend some time at a museum before heading back to Cairo for your evening meal.

Day 5

This final day takes travellers to Khartoum, which is one of the fastest growing cities in Africa. After exploring the city, take a boat down the Nile to Cairo. This is a great way to end your trip as you enjoy a relaxing sail down this river.

Weekend Itinerary

Day 1:

- One of the seven wonders of the ancient world is the Giza Pyramid complex.
- Discover the Great Sphinx, a huge limestone figure with a lion's body and a human head.
- Explore the nearby Khan el-Khalili bazaar, a renowned shopping area with a wide variety

of vendors offering anything from spices to souvenirs.

Day 2:

- Visit the Egyptian Museum, which has a sizable collection of mummies and antiquities from ancient Egypt.
- Enjoy the breathtaking sights and vistas by taking a sail along the Nile River.
- Visit the Cairo Citadel, a historic Islamic stronghold that provides fantastic city views.

One Week Itinerary

Day 1-2: Cairo

- Visit the Great Sphinx and the Giza Pyramids.
- Go shopping at the Khan el-Khalili bazaar.
- the Egyptian Museum visit.
- Embark on a Nile River cruise.
- Visit the Citadel of Cairo.

Day 3: Alexandria

- Visit Alexandria, a historic city on the Mediterranean coast, for a day excursion.
- Visit the Bibliotheca Alexandrina, a contemporary library situated where the Library of Alexandria once stood.
- Discover the Citadel of Qaitbay, a fortification from the 15th century with stunning views of the ocean.
- Visit the Roman Amphitheater, a historic venue with room for up to 800 spectators.

Day 4-5: Luxor

- Fly to Luxor, a city located on the Nile River's east bank.
- One of the biggest ancient religious sites in the world is the Karnak Temple Complex.
- Discover the Valley of the Kings, where pharaohs and their wives are interred.
- Visit the Luxor Temple, a sizable temple from ancient Egypt built in honor of Amun.

Day 6-7: Aswan

- To reach Aswan, an Egyptian city on the Nile River, take a train or a car.
- Visit the Philae Temple, a stunning historic structure to the goddess Isis.
- Investigate the Aswan High Dam, a stunning engineering achievement that manages the Nile's flow.

- Take a boat journey to the Elephantine Island, a historic site that provides fantastic views of the river and the area around it.

9 Day Itinerary

Day 1-2: Cairo

- Visit the Great Sphinx and the Giza Pyramids.
- Go shopping at the Khan el-Khalili bazaar.
- the Egyptian Museum visit.
- Embark on a Nile River cruise.
- Visit the Citadel of Cairo.

Day 3-4: Alexandria

- Visit Alexandria, a historic city on the Mediterranean coast, for a day excursion.
- Visit the Bibliotheca Alexandrina, a contemporary library situated where the Library of Alexandria once stood.

- Discover the Citadel of Qaitbay, a fortification from the 15th century with stunning views of the ocean.
- Visit the Roman Amphitheater, a historic venue with room for up to 800 spectators.

Day 5-7: Siwa Oasis

- Visit the Siwa Oasis, a secluded desert oasis renowned for its breathtaking natural surroundings, after a long drive.
- Visit the Shali Fortress, a historic fortification made of mud bricks that previously served as the Siwan neighborhood's hub.
- Investigate the Cleopatra's Pool, a natural spring where the fabled monarch is rumored to have taken a bath.
- View the Amun-dedicated ancient temple known as the Temple of the Oracle.

Day 8-9: Marsa Alam

- Take a plane to the Red Sea vacation city of Marsa Alam.
- Take advantage of some of the best diving and snorkeling in the world, featuring vibrant coral reefs and a bounty of aquatic life.

Chapter 8: Accommodations in Egypt

Egypt has a wide range of housing choices, from expensive resorts and hotels to guesthouses and motels that are affordable. Some of the top locations to stay in Egypt are the ones listed below:

Cairo: The main city and the political and cultural hub of Egypt is Cairo. It provides a range of lodging choices, including upscale hotels, boutique hotels, and affordable lodging. Some of the nicest places to stay in Cairo are the Fairmont Nile City, Le Meridian Pyramids Hotel and Spa, and Four Seasons Hotel Cairo at Nile Plaza.

Luxor: The beautiful and historic city of Luxor is situated beside the Nile River. It is well-known for its many historical sights, including the ruins of Luxor and Karnak, and it provides a range of housing alternatives, including luxurious hotels, traditional guesthouses, and affordable hotels. The Hlton Luxury Resort and Spa, the Sofitel Winter Palace Luxor, and the Steigenberger Nile Palace Luxor are some of the best places to stay in the city.

Aswan: On the banks of the Nile River in southern Egypt, the picturesque and active city of Aswan may be found. It is well recognized for its breathtaking environment, which includes the Temple of Phlege and the Aswan High Dam, and it provides a range of housing alternatives, including luxurious hotels, traditional inns, and affordable hotels. The greatest places to stay in Asawan include the Old Catarac Hotel, Movenpick Resort Asawan, and Nile Valley Hotel.

Hurghada: On Egypt's Red Sea coast, the town of Hurghada is a well-known beach resort. It offers a range of housing options, such as luxurious hotels, beach resorts, and affordable guesthouses. It is highly recognized for its stunning beaches, world-class diving, and snorkeling. It also has crystal clear waters. The Hilton Hurghada Resort, the Marriott Hurghada Resort, and the Novotel Hurghada Hotel are the best places to stay in the city.

Sharm El Sheikh: The well-known beach resort town of Sharm El Sheikh is located at the southernmost point of the Sinai Peninsula. The stunning beaches, top-notch diving and snorkeling, and vibrant nightlife are well renowned for this destination. There are several places to stay, including luxury hotels, seaside resorts, and affordable guesthouses. The Four Seasons Resort Sharm El Sheikh, Hilton Sharm El Sheikh Bay Resort, and Hyatt Regency Sharm El Sheikh are some of the best places to stay in the city. Generally speaking, depending on your interests and budget, Egypt offers a wide selection of lovely hotels. Whether you're seeking for elegance, comfort, or affordability in your housing, Egypt has a wide range of options.

Best Hotels in Egypt

Depending on your preferences and price range, Egypt boasts a large range of good hotels. Some of Egypt's top hotels include the ones listed below:

The Four Seasons Hotel Cairo at Nile Plaza offers luxurious suites with breathtaking Nile River views. It is located right in the middle of Cairo. The hotel provides opulent guest rooms and suites, as well as a number of dining options, a spa, and a rooftop pool with panoramic city views.

The Le Meridian Pyramids Hotel and Spa, which provides opulent lodging and easy access to some of Egypt's most famous monuments, is near to the Giza Pyramids. In addition to several dining options, a spa, and an outdoor pool with sweeping views of the palaces, the hotel provides opulent guest rooms and suites.

The Fairmont Nebraska City offers luxurious accommodation and easy access to the city's top sights. It is located in Caero's center. The hotel features opulent guest rooms and suites, a number of dining establishments, a spa, and a rooftop pool with mesmerizing views of the city and the Nile River.

The Hilton Luxor Resort and Spa, offers opulent lodging and easy access to some of Egypt's most well-known sites. It is situated on the banks of the Nile River. Popular guest rooms and suites, a selection of dining establishments, a spa, and an outdoor pool with breathtaking views of the Nile River and the surrounding area are all available at the hotel.

The magnificent hotel Sofitel Winter Some of Egypt's most well-known landmarks are conveniently close to Palace Luxor. It may be found in the center of Luxor. Along with offering a range of dining options, the hotel's amenities include a spa and a pool that looks out into the surrounding countryside. Luxurious lodging with easy access to some of Egypt's most famous attractions can be found at the Steenburger Nile Palace Luxor. On the Nile River's banks is where it is located. A spa and a swimming pool with views of the nearby countryside are among the hotel's attractions, in addition to a selection of eating choices.

The perfect hotel for you will depend on your interests, your budget, and the sights and activities you intend to experience while you're there. Egypt boasts a wide variety of outstanding hotels.

How to Get Around in Egypt

Depending on where you're going and what you prefer, there are many various ways to travel in Egypt. Following are a few of the most popular modes of transportation in Egypt:

By taxi: In Egypt, taxes are a common and useful method of exchange. A cab can be called on the street or reserved in advance through a taxi company. It is a good practice to haggle the fare up front to avoid any misunderstandings, even if Egyptian taxes are commonly metered.

By Car: If you want to see Egypt at your own pace, renting a car is a great option. A valid driver's license and an international driving licence are required in order to rent a car from one of the many car rental firms in the nation. To help you negotiate Egypt's occasionally hectic traffic, it is advised to utilize a GPS navigation system or hire a local driver.

By bus: Egypt may be easily and cheaply navigated via buses. The Egyptian National Authority for Tunnels (NAT) oversees the nation's public transit network, which connects to a number of key cities and well-liked tourist hotspots. Due to the frequent crowding and potential lack of air conditioning in Egyptian enterprises, it is a good idea to bring water and plan your trip in advance.

By train: It is practical and economical to use the train between Egypt's major cities. Lines are provided to various key towns and popular tourist destinations by Egyptian National Railways (ENR), which oversees the nation's rail network. Most trains in Egypt are dependable and comfortable, with amenities like air conditioning and dining cars.

By boat: In order to reach between cities and popular tourist spots, boat travel along the Nile River is a frequent and practical choice. Public ferries, conventional flotilla boats, and well-known cruise ships are just a few of the various kinds of watercraft that are readily available.

The majority of Egyptian boats are aesthetically pleasing and provide a distinctive and gorgeous appearance as a mode of transportation. You have a variety of ways to learn about Egypt in general, and the ideal one for you will depend on your financial objectives, financial circumstances, and personal preferences. To get the most out of your trip, it's a good idea to thoroughly organize your trips and do your homework beforehand.

Chapter 9: Egypt's Hidden Gems

The tourist industry in Egypt has great potential and is a significant employer in the country's economy. The nation enjoys several advantages, including an agreeable climate, a lengthy and rich history and tradition, amiable and welcoming people, a good location near its important European and Arab tourist markets, and a diversified and beautiful natural environment. We discover that Egypt is so much more than its more limited, typical marquee attractions as we travel throughout the nation.

Egypt has long been known for its beaches, diving, Luxor, Aswan, and Cairo (which attracts both European and Arab tourists). We cover each of Egypt's six regions, which are all unquestionably essential.

1) The nature-rich northwest,
2) The lively northeast,

3) The intriguing Western Desert oases,
4) The majestic Nile Valley (Middle and Upper Egypt, south of Cairo),
5) The scenic Red Sea region, and
6) The versatile Sinai Peninsula

Including well-known and, in particular, underestimated attractions as well as creative ideas for a worldwide, thriving, and environmentally sustainable tourism business.

There are many hidden gems to be explored in Egypt. These places are often completely unknown to tourists, but are full of history and provide a unique experience to those who take the time to go.

The Coptic Quarter

Despite the fact that tourists frequently ignore it, Cairo's Coptic Quarter is a hidden gem that is highly recommended. It is located in Old Cairo, also referred to as Coptic Cairo, and is one of the oldest Christian neighborhoods in the city.

The Coptic Quarter is home to a number of historic churches and monasteries, including The Hanging Church, one of Cairo's oldest and most notable churches. The church's name comes from the fact that it is built on the gatehouse of a Roman stronghold and features excellent paintings, icons, and woodwork.

Visitors to the Coptic Quarter can also enjoy the Coptic Museum, which houses exhibits on the history of Christianity in Egypt and has artifacts from the early Christian era such manuscripts, textiles, and icons. A number of storied roads and alleyways can also be found in the region, including the well-known "Street of the Tentmakers," where visitors may watch artisans creating classic Egyptian tapestries and fabrics. To really appreciate the Coptic Quarter, visitors need plan to spend numerous hours seeing the various churches, museums, and historic streets. Consider taking a tour with an informed local guide to gain a deeper understanding of the region's cultural and historical significance. Visitors should be aware that the community places a high value on religion and should dress modestly. The Coptic Quarter may become congested during the peak seasons of the year, so visitors should make adequate plans.

The City of the Dead

El Arafa, also referred to as the City of the Dead, is a mysterious and distinctive hidden gem in Cairo that attracts very few tourists. This vast necropolis, spanning several kilometers, has hundreds of thousands of tombs, mausoleums, and burial chambers. Despite its dreary exterior, the City of the Dead is a bustling neighborhood with many families using the tombs as temporary homes. Visitors have the choice of wandering the area's narrow lanes and paths, examining the tombs' amazing carvings and patterns, or even going inside some of the more elaborate mausoleums.

The Mosque of In Tulun, one of Cairo's oldest and most beautiful mosques, is among the notable mosques that can be found in the City of the Dead. Another site open to tourists is the Beit El Sehemy, a restored 18th-century house with distinctive Islamic architecture and design.

To really appreciate the City of the Dead, visitors need be prepared to spend numerous hours touring the various tombs, mosques, and ancient buildings. Consider taking a tour with a knowledgeable local guide to gain a deeper appreciation of the region's cultural and historical significance.

The sombre atmosphere of the location should be respected, and visitors should be mindful of local traditions and customs. Travelers should make proper planning because the City of the Dead could be crowded during the busiest travel season.

The Street Art of Downtown Cairo

The street art in Downtown Cairo is a vibrant and dynamic hidden gem that showcases the city's aesthetic and cultural individuality. The area is renowned for its amazing graffiti and murals, which can be found on buildings, walls, and alleyways.

Street art in Downtown Cairo features a wide range of themes and styles, including political and social critique, cultural allusions, and pop culture references. Many of the murals, which reflect the unique perspectives and experiences of Cairo's residents, were created by local artists.

There is a self-directed walking tour of the street art in Downtown Cairo as well as expert-led guided excursions. The guided tours offer a unique viewpoint on the city's contemporary art scene as well as its social and political landscape.

One of the most famous pieces of street art in Downtown Cairo is the "Mohamed Mahmoud Wall," which is made up of a number of stirring political murals that depict the 2011 Egyptian Revolution and the struggle for social justice.

Two more notable murals are the colorful "Famous Faces of Cairo" painting, which recognizes the status of women in Egyptian society, and the "Graffiti Women" mural, which features significant Egyptian individuals.

To really enjoy the street art in Downtown Cairo, visitors need plan on spending a lot of time exploring the various murals and graffiti art across the neighborhood. They should also appreciate the artwork, the artists who created it, as well as the regional traditions and customs.

The Cairo Food Markets

Cairo's souks, or food markets, are a hidden gem that offer visitors a unique and authentic gastronomic experience. Spices, fruits, vegetables, meats, and sweets are among the many regional and local delights that can be obtained in the markets, which are scattered around the city.

In Cairo's food markets, tourists can sample traditional Egyptian cuisine like ful medames, a hearty dish composed of fava beans, garlic, and lemon juice, or koshary, a well-known street snack made of rice, pasta, lentils, and fried onions. Enjoy sweet treats like baklava, a pastry made from layers of phyllo dough and honey syrup, or konafa, a sweet cheese pastry coated with syrup.

Along with the food, the markets are a sensory experience because of the colorful produce displays, the aromas of spices and freshly baked bread, and the sounds of vendors shouting at customers.

Two of Cairo's favorite food markets include the Khan El-Khalili Bazaar, which offers a wide variety of street food and snacks, and the Al-Ataba Market, which is renowned for its fresh produce and seafood. Other, lesser-known markets may also be found all over the city, giving tourists a more intimate and real glimpse into the way of life there.

To really experience Cairo's food markets, visitors should plan to spend many hours exploring the countless booths and dealers while sampling a variety of local treats. Along with respecting local traditions and practices, like negotiating with sellers, they must also be gracious to the merchants and their wares.

The Royal Jewelry Museum

A little-known gem that offers tourists a fascinating glimpse into the opulence and beauty of Egypt's royal past is the Royal Jewelry Museum in Alexandria's Zizenia area. The magnificent neoclassical palace where the museum is now housed was formerly home to King Farouk, the final pharaoh of Egypt.

The museum is home to a sizable collection of heirloom jewelry and personal items belonging to the royal family, including ornate necklaces, bracelets, tiaras, and brooches as well as timepieces, cigarette boxes, and other antiques. A number of the pieces on display are extremely significant both historically and aesthetically, and they are adorned with priceless gems including diamonds, emeralds, and rubies.

One of the highlights of the museum is Queen Farida's jewelry collection, who was King Farouk's first wife. The collection includes a stunning necklace composed of diamonds and emeralds, as well as different diamond and sapphire tiaras and other pieces.

Visit the Royal Jewelry Museum and take a look around the opulent palace's interiors, which have been lovingly restored to their former splendor. The palace features intricate woodwork, marble floors, and decorative ceilings. Additionally, it includes a nice garden and a patio outside with a stunning view of the Mediterranean Sea.

Visitors to the Royal Jewelry Museum should plan on spending a lot of time looking over the museum's collection and admiring the stunning palace interiors.

Egypt's Red Sea

Another hidden gem in Egypt is located along the country's Red Sea coastline. The modern city of Sharm El Sheikh has several picturesque beaches, which are a popular tourist destination. Nearby is the ancient city of Siwa, which is home to some of Egypt's most impressive archaeological sites. One of these sites, the Temple of Hercules, contains a statue of the Greek god.

The Museum Ship

Another popular site that has excellent views over the Red Sea is the island of Elephantine. This small island was excavated in 1960 by a French archaeologist and holds an impressive collection of artifacts. One of these is the Rosetta Stone, which was discovered in Egypt and became a historical artifact because it contained a detailed translation of several ancient Egyptian hieroglyphs.

The Strait of Tiran

The last hidden gem in Egypt is located just off the coast on the Gulf of Suez. The Strait of Tiran was cut through solid rock when it was created. This formation has a long history and is still used today as an important shipping lane for vessels traveling between Egypt and Asia.

Ancient Egypt

Egypt is located in the northern region of Africa. It is considered to be one of the cradles of civilization and is home to many ancient sites. The pyramids at Giza are among the most well-known structures in the world, and they are also one of the Seven Wonders of the Ancient World. As it flows through Egypt, the Nile River serves as a source of water as well as rich soil for farming. Visitors to Egypt can take a leisurely boat ride down the Nile or visit the nation's numerous museums and archaeological sites. Egypt has much to offer everyone, whether they are interested in ancient history or contemporary culture.

Chapter 10: Great pyramid

Cheops' Pyramid. The only one of the seven wonders of the ancient world that is still standing, it is the oldest of the pyramids.

Cheops, the fourth dynasty pharaoh, gave the order for its construction, which was completed in 2570 BC.

For 3,800 years, it held the record for the highest structure on Earth before Lincoln Cathedral in England overtook it in the 14th century.

Khufu's pyramid was constructed in the northeastern region of the Giza Plateau, at its highest point, to ensure that it would be clearly visible from a long distance.

Akhet Khufu (The Horizon of Khufu).

About 40 kilometers away from the pyramid his father Sneferu erected in Dashur, Khufu chose the Giza region to construct his monument.

He created a level platform on the rock itself where the pyramid is located to minimize tilting.

Only a few slabs of the white Tura limestone that once covered it are still present at the pyramid's base.

It had a wall surrounding it and a pavement 10 meters wide on all sides.

On the north side, very little pavement is still present.

The chamber beneath the ground was never finished.

Through a little corridor, you can get there.

Blocks of red stone line the king's room. Five discharge chambers are located above the hall, each with a sloping roof to evenly distribute the structure's weight.

A total of 2.3 million stone blocks, with an average weight of 2.5 tons and some exceeding 70 tons, were used in its construction. Prior to a 14th-century earthquake that partially uprooted the coating, it was coated by almost 27,000 exquisitely polished white limestone blocks. After that, it was used to create Cairo's buildings.

The king's chamber, the queen's chamber, and the basement chamber are the pyramid's three principal chambers.

The chambers are entered from the north side by a descending route that connects to two additional passages: one ascends to the Great Gallery, and the other descends to the basement chamber. Both passageways are blocked at their ends by enormous granite stones.

Great gallery

Its length is 47 meters, and its height is 8 meters. From the ground to a height of two meters, the walls are vertical; from that point to the ceiling, they form a false vault.

The King's Chamber

It features a rectangular floor plan, smooth walls and a plain ceiling without any decorations. Since it is wider than the passageways, it was dumped there during the construction of the pyramid. The unloading chambers are on the roof. They keep the roof from being loaded down with the entire weight of the building. Through the antechamber, one enters the actual chamber.

The Queen's Chamber

The so-called queen's room was built to house a statue of the pharaoh rather than the king's wife (spiritual representation of the deceased).

It is situated on the pyramid's axis. A corridor through the lower portion of the Great Gallery leads to it.

The underground chamber

It was discovered in the subsoil and consists of a well, a short gallery, and two rooms that resemble sarcophagi. It can be reached via a descending route and a small, almost vertical tunnel that is punctured in the bricks of the Great Gallery.

Ventilation channels

Due to its current function as ventilation channels, each royal chamber has two tiny, incline ducts that exit on the north and south walls. Because the queen's chamber's channels were blocked off from the exterior by the thick slabs of lining, it is uncertain what they originally did.

Dimensions of the Great Pyramid

146.5 meters tall at first (current height: 136 meters). 230 meters are the length of each side.

The huge pyramid is the culmination of a process of developing building methods that started during the reign of Dyeser and continued during Seneferu.

The Greek historian Herodotus relates what the Egyptian priests told him in his account of how the pyramids were constructed, making it the earliest source to do so (450 BC).

The carved stones were hoisted from tier to tier using objects made of short logs, from top to bottom, during the 20 years it took to build.

Some archaeologists agreed with these assertions, but others suggested using wide ramps that were parallel to the face, or by an external ramp that rose to a height of 45 meters, followed from there by another spiral-shaped inside ramp. None of these theories has been proven true to this day.

According to Breyndeback's book Travels from 1484, some people think they are the granaries that Joseph erected in Egypt, while others think they are massive sundials or sand-blocking structures.

The first person to assert that it was the pharaoh's tomb was John Greaves in 1638.

During his expedition in Egypt in 1798, Napoleon paid a visit to the King's Chamber.

Chapter 11: Top Places To Visit

1. Cairo

Cairo is one of those cities that has something to offer everyone, no matter what kind of traveler you are. If you don't mind the crowds, this renowned tourist spot, which is frequently ranked among the busiest in the world, is the ideal site to learn about Egyptian history and culture.

History & Culture

Cairo has had "recent" development in comparison to much of Egypt. Although it was established in 969 CE close to the Nile Delta, the city's modern history actually began in the fourth century AD with the construction of a Roman fortification called Babylon, which was far later than the construction of Memphis, the ancient capital, and the pyramids. The oldest building in the current city of Cairo, this fortress is still standing.

Cairo was expanding and changing up until the 14th century, when the plague struck and killed some 200,000 people. The 15th century was not much better, as early Ottoman authority gradually reduced the city's political and economic power. Cairo's prominence increased dramatically in succeeding centuries, elevating it to the status of one of the most important and affluent cities in Africa and the Middle East.

The background of religious history in Cairo is very fascinating. Coptic Christianity, which is still the name given to Christians in Egypt, was centered there. Nowadays, almost all Egyptians practice Sunni Islam, and foreign visitors to Cairo may clearly feel this, if only because there are so many enormous, ancient mosques.

The Egyptian Museum

Attractions & Activities

Cairo has many other sights besides the Pyramids that you really must see. The Egyptian Museum is the first of these locations, and even those who loathe museums will find it enjoyable. With its elaborate coffins, historic buildings, and spectacular items just waiting to be uncovered, Cairo's Egyptian Museum will offer you a taste of Egypt's amazing history.

Take a trip through the Citadel and Mosque of Muhammad Ali for an insight into Egypt's Muslim past. One of Cairo's most gorgeous structures, this breathtaking mosque was constructed in 1848, and it is just a short stroll from the Egyptian Museum. Arms and legs need to be covered if you want to enter.

Visit the Khan El Khalili bazaar to receive a colorful glimpse of Cairo's bustling market life. It is Cairo's largest and best market, and visiting it will make you feel as though you have been transported to an ancient Arab souk. Here, you can try your trading abilities and find clothing, jewelry, lamps, tea, and a variety of other goods.

Finally, visit Coptic Cairo to see how the city's minority Christian community lives. It is a historical site that depicts the origins of the faith in Egypt and has a museum as well as a number of opulent churches. As you wander this neighborhood, you'll have a strong sense that you've been transported back in time.

Sharm El Sheikh

This city on the Sinai Peninsula, sometimes called the "City of Peace," is located as far south as it can go without actually touching the Red Sea. There are only 35,000 individuals living there, which is a small population compared to Cairo's 10 million. Sharm El Sheikh (or "Sharm," as the locals call it) is now a well-liked resort city and tourist attraction, and because of its position, it is a hotspot for scuba diving and other water sports.

History & Culture

The entire Sinai Peninsula is made up of a vast mountain range that ends in a level desert. People who visit this location for the first time frequently describe the desert-sea combination as bizarre.

In 1967, when it was under Israeli occupation, Sharm El Sheikh began to see a large increase in tourist numbers. Israel left after Egypt and Israel signed peace accords in the late 1970s, but the growth of this region continued. It now has everything a tourist might need, including a Hard Rock Cafe.

Due to the present unrest in Egypt, tourists have recently developed a distinct preference for Sharm El Sheikh. Many tourists have been urged to avoid Cairo and instead stay in the security of resorts. 9,000 Britons can currently be spotted in Sharm El Sheikh every day. People travel to the area for various reasons, including sunbathing on the beach and having adventures in the Red Sea.

Ras Mohammed Reef

Attractions & Activities

Sharm El Sheikh is a popular diving location, as was already noted. In this resort town, that really is the only thing to do. The Red Sea's underwater environment is renowned for being extremely vivid and colorful. Within a two-hour boat journey of Sharm El Sheikh are two of the world's top diving destinations: the Tiran Reef and Ras Mohammed Reef.

A desert safari is an additional choice, and it appears exactly as you would expect. You can travel the safari route through the Sinai desert on a Jeep, a camel, or your own two feet. You can explore some breathtaking canyons and mountains, but make sure you select a knowledgeable and responsible guide.

There are countless alternatives available in Sharm El Sheikh if you can't get enough of adventure sports; parasailing, quad biking, go-karting, and horseback riding are all well-liked by tourists.

2. Dahab

Dahab was once a sleepy fishing village but has now developed into a bustling tourist destination that has thrived since the early 1980s, much like Hurghada (and many other Egyptian tourist destinations). Dahab, which lies 80 kilometers northeast of Sharm El Sheikh, is a different location well-known for its Red Sea diving prospects.

History & Culture

There are numerous reasons for the name "Dahab." The gold that flowed down from the mountains in the desert is possibly why the word in Egyptian Arabic literally translates to "gold." Those who disagree claim that the term derives from the hue of the sand found nearby Dahab. Locals frequently have their own interpretations of the name's origins, frequently claiming that it refers to the color of the sky in Dahab after sunset.

But the conversation doesn't end there. Another tale that is frequently told by locals offers a different explanation for the name. Dahab experiences significant flooding every few years as a result of an increase in mountain storms that send more water into the sea than usual. The stormy bay turns gold as a result of the aggravating sand brought down by this surge of water from the mountains.

There is yet another tale, told by the local Bedouin. They gave the location the name "Waqaat Thahaab" when their people came. According to legend, this place's nice surroundings caused people to lose track of time, hence the moniker "time goes." The name of the town eventually merely became "Thahaab," which is readily confused by foreigners with "Dahab."

Whatever the name's origins, it is certain that this place has long been a source of pleasure and beauty.

Windsurfing in Dahab

Attractions & Activities

In Dahab, there are countless opportunities for outdoor recreation. The dives here are great for experienced divers, but beginners are encouraged to go elsewhere for their first diving experience. Dahab is home to The Canyon, another well-known international scuba diving attraction, as well as "the world's most dangerous diving site," known as the Blue Hole. Divers travel from all around the world to enjoy these difficult dive sites.

Dahab is renowned for having outstanding windsurfing in addition to diving and snorkeling. It receives more consistent wind than Red Sea coast rivals Hurghada and Sharm El Sheikh, making it the perfect location for windsurfers.

There are several activities on land as well as additional water sports that are generally accessible. Activities worth trying in Dahab include camel riding, horseback riding, cycling, mountain biking, Jeep excursions, and quad bike excursions. Each year, new activities emerge, expanding the range of activities available to tourists.

3. Luxor

The name Luxor, which translates to "the palaces," makes it a paradise for history buffs as you can see a staggering amount of Thebes' ancient ruins just by strolling through the city. Thebes is considered to be one of the world's greatest open-air museums, and it is the main reason that thousands of tourists visit the magnificent city of Luxor each year.

History & Culture

Thebes, the ancient Egyptian capital city that served as the center of the New Kingdom, was situated where Luxor is today. The name of the city has changed a lot over time. Ancient Egyptian literature frequently mention Thebes, referring to it as the "city of the sceptre" or "the temple." It was sometimes referred to as "southern Heliopolis" and "the city of the hundred gates." Like every area with numerous names and monikers, Luxor has played a crucial role in human history.

In the Eleventh Dynasty, which started some time about 2134 BC, it developed into a prosperous metropolis. It earned notoriety as a center of luxury and social supremacy, as well as of art, religion, politics, and wisdom. As time passed, the city's wealth and political influence increased. Up until Alexandria replaced it in the Late Period, it served as the political center of the world (664 BC - 332 BC). Despite this setback, Thebes continued to serve as the religious center of Egypt, and neighboring Karnak was home to Egypt's most significant temple—built for the god Amon-Ra, king of the gods.

The city's eventual destruction by the Assyrian emperor further accelerated its tendency of declining in importance on the political and economic fronts. The main industry in Luxor, a modern city that was constructed over Thebes' ruins, is tourism.

Karnak Temple

Attractions & Activities

On the western side of the Nile are the ancient remains of Thebes, whereas the majority of the modern city of Luxor is situated on the eastern bank. However, more hotels have recently popped up on the western side of the river, making it possible to spend the night there. Typically, tourists stay on the eastern side and cross the river for day trips.

Even so, it could be a good idea to spend the night on the eastern side because it has more lodging options for visitors and is home to more stores, eateries, motels, and public transportation hubs.

Luxor offers almost too many sights to see. The main attractions include all of the temple ruins, such as Luxor Temple and Karnak Temple, as well as a number of museums, including as the Mummification Museum and Luxor Museum, which will educate and astonish any visitor.

The Valley of the Kings and the Valley of the Queens, Medinet Habu, the Ramesseum, the Noble Tombs, Deir el-Bahri, Malkata, and the Colossi of Memnon are some of the top sights to see on the western bank.

4. Giza

Giza, Egypt's main tourist destination, is home to some of the most stunning ancient structures in existence, including the Great Sphinx, the Great Pyramid of Giza, as well as a number of other sizable pyramids and temples. The Giza plateau, where the three pyramids stand, is unexpectedly close to the suburban metropolis of Giza, which provides a hazy backdrop to the bustling city. The Giza plateau is unquestionably one of the oldest and most well-known tourist destinations in the world.

History & Culture

Construction on the Great Pyramid of Giza took place in just 30 years. The Great Pyramid, together with two other pyramids, the Sphinx, and other structures on the Giza plateau, gaze out over the west bank of the Nile. Giza served as the location for the royal dead's final resting place five millennia ago. As a result, it was constructed close to Memphis, the former capital of Egypt.

The Great Pyramid was constructed in 2550 B.C. to serve as King Khufu's tomb. The Pharaoh of the fourth dynasty himself ordered the construction of the pyramid, perhaps aware that it would take many years. Its construction required millions of stone blocks, each weighing roughly 2.5 tons, which is an amazing achievement for the time period.

How precisely did they transport these enormous blocks, the biggest of which weight a whopping nine tons each, from hundreds of miles distant without the aid of modern technology? It is still unable to provide a definitive solution to the question.

Khafre, the son of Khufu, constructed the Sphinx and a second pyramid after the Great Pyramid. The third and last pyramid in Giza was constructed by Menkaure, who historians believe to be Khafre's son.

The City of Giza

Attractions & Activities

Although the Giza Plateau is famous across the world, it is not because it is a contemporary, vibrant suburb of Cairo. It is not surprising that people swarm to Giza to witness the last of the Seven Ancient Wonders of the World.

The Giza Necropolis, which is another name for a cemetery, is the name of this UNESCO monument. It consists of the Great Sphinx of Giza and the three pyramids, all of which can be visited on your own, as part of a guided tour, or with a private car and guide. Even a camel tour of Giza is a possibility!

You might also visit Memphis, the site of ancient Egypt's capital, where visitors can stroll through the remnants of Rameses II's pillared hall, as part of a tour of the region.

During the peak tourist season, aggressive salespeople that stand around the foot of the pyramids will undoubtedly be present when you visit the Giza pyramids. If someone offers to snap your photo, proceed with extreme caution because they will undoubtedly want a sizable gratuity. It is well worth the additional money to enter one of the pyramids. Claustrophobics may wish to wait outdoors as it does contain some small places.

5. Hurghada

Hurghada, which was once a little fishing community, has advanced considerably because of the tourism sector. It is currently one of the most well-liked beach resorts in the entire country of Egypt, known for its scuba diving options and several hotels lining the beachfront. Due to its proximity to Luxor, hundreds of visitors combine trips to the two places each year, ensuring the success of this lovely resort town. Both beachgoers and explorers are drawn there by its Red Sea coast position.

History & Culture

Hurghada was once a fishing village in the early 1900s, making it a very young city in Egyptian perspective. The city first began to realize its full potential in the 1980s, when a wave of Egyptian and foreign investors contributed to a rapid increase in the city's population and a thriving tourism sector.

This coastal resort city is becoming a tourist destination of dreams for people traveling there to unwind: warm weather, gorgeous beaches, opulent hotels, and a vibrant nightlife are just a few of its many attractions.

Whether they are fisherman or snorkelers, water enthusiasts have long been drawn to Hurghada. Sailboarding, yachting, scuba diving, jet skiing, parasailing, and windsurfing are the most popular water activities presently.

Hurghada is not the place to go if you're hoping to see how an average Egyptian lives. Particularly during the winter holidays, it is inundated with tourists, the most of which are from Germany, Russia, and Italy. Even Egyptian tourists enjoy traveling here for a few days of fun and relaxation. Due to its perpetually dry and warm climate, where temperatures of around 30 degrees Celsius are the norm, Hurghada hardly has a peak season.

Mahmya Beach

Attractions & Activities

Near Hurghada, you can engage in almost any water sport, but scuba diving and snorkeling are by far the most common. The Red Sea's coral reefs are strikingly colorful, and a wide diversity of tropical fish can be found there.

Beginner divers will find Hurghada to be especially user-friendly. Local divers have experience instructing novices. It won't be hard to find a diving escort or guided diving adventure, nor will it be particularly expensive. Let the excursions begin by asking your hotel to connect you with one.

If you'd rather have adventures on dry land, you may have just as much fun riding motorbikes or beach buggies in the nearby desert. If you're feeling particularly daring, you could even ride a quad over the Sahara Desert to have tea with a Bedouin clan.

Additionally, for some breathtaking vistas, you can ride a camel through the biblical plains. Or you might travel by boat to the isolated Big and Little Giftun islands. At case you didn't get the point, Hurghada offers a wide range of interesting activities, making it impossible for you to justifiably stay in your hotel.

6. Aswan

Aswan, an additional well-liked vacation spot with a more relaxed, tranquil vibe, is situated on the banks of the Nile in southern Egypt. After visiting other Nile city stops like Luxor and Cairo, it's a perfect area for travellers to relax and take a breather. With its own ancient remains and a population of only about 275,000, it is a tiny replica of other, busier Egyptian cities.

History & Culture

Aswan has had an unexpected, crucial impact on Egypt's history for a little city. In the past, the city of Aswan was referred to as Swenett, after an Egyptian deity. Swenett was regarded as the entrance to Africa or the start of Egypt.

Due to its advantageous location for gaining access to the Nile delta, it was the first settlement to be established in the entire nation. It was once famous for its granite quarries, which supplied all of Egypt with the syenite used to build numerous ancient Egyptian structures, such as the Pyramids.

Every ruling dynasty in the history of Egypt used Swenett as a garrison town, making it significant militarily as well. Because of its location in the south, it was employed in wars against Nubia in particular (previously called Kush). Swenett was also in charge of obtaining tolls and customs from boats entering and leaving the Nile.

Today, there are many Nubians living in Aswan, and the west bank is home to several peaceful Nubian settlements.

Philae Temple

Attractions & Activities

The ideal location to learn more about Nubia and the Nubian people is Aswan. A thirty minute stroll from the city center will bring you to the Nubian Museum, which houses an astonishing collection of Nubian artifacts. Although you shouldn't count on the employees there to be very helpful with your inquiries, the museum is set up well enough for you to appreciate it without a guide. Try taking a water taxi to the Elephantine Island to visit the Nubian villages of Siou and Koti for a more genuine understanding of the culture. Several spectacular temples can be seen here, along with the Aswan Museum.

The Fatimid Cemetery is located in southern Aswan and provides insight into the now-decayed Fatimid empire. The world's largest ancient obelisk, the Unfinished Obelisk, is located across the street. Take a walk down the Kornish Al Nile thereafter; it's pleasant on its own and leads to the Ferial Gardens, which are open to exploring for free.

You might be interested in Kitcheners Island and Seheyl Island, two other islands. A 6.8-hectare botanical garden featuring animals, flowers, and trees may be found in the first location. In addition to the Famine Stela, a hieroglyphic inscription from the 18th dynasty etched on the side of a rock, Seheyl Island is known for its beaded jewelry.

However, there's still more! The Philae Temple, which was formerly on Agilkia Island but is currently situated on the edge of Lake Nasser, is probably the most well-known attraction in Aswan. It was established in 362 BC and presently hosts a nighttime light and sound extravaganza.

7. Alexandria

Alexandria is Egypt's second largest city, although with only 5 million inhabitants, it appears insignificant in contrast. Alexandria was founded by and named for Alexander the Great. The former vibrant, cosmopolitan capital city today draws tourists primarily for its historical and cultural features. Through the city's new façade, visitors can catch a glimpse of the past. Greek, French, and Roman features may all be found if you look hard because each invasion gave rise to new architectural styles.

History & Culture

Alexander the Great, who gave Alexandria its name, established it in 331 BC. The majestic Lighthouse of Alexandria, also known as Pharos, served as a symbol of the city's legendary prominence and splendor. The Pyramids of Giza were the tallest structures on Earth when Ptolemy I constructed this fabled lighthouse in the third century BC. It was also one of the Seven Wonders of the Ancient World for good reason.

If the Alexandria Lighthouse wasn't enough, there was also the Library of Alexandria, which was by far the biggest library at the period. In fact, it was built in the third century BC, much before the Lighthouse of Alexandria. This library was frequently traversed by scientists and philosophers seeking knowledge and exchanging views. The best academics of the day, including Archimedes and Hipparchus, came to study at the Musaeum of Alexandria, which it was a part of.

Until the Arabs conquered Egypt in 641 CE and decided to make Cairo their capital, Alexandria remained a brilliant center of learning and reputation. According to experts, this is the time the library was destroyed. The lighthouse was destroyed by two significant earthquakes hundreds of years later, in the 14th century CE.

Although Alexandria lost some of its former power, it remained an important trading harbor for hundreds of years. Alexandria was repeatedly captured, destroyed, and rebuilt throughout the ages. It is now the second-largest city in Egypt and a very well-liked tourist attraction.

Library of Alexandria

Attractions & Activities

In Alexandria, there are almost too many historical sites to count. Let's start with the Citadel of Qaitbay, which was initially constructed in 1477 CE but has since been repeatedly destroyed and rebuilt. It was formerly a city guardian and was purposefully constructed on the precise spot where the Lighthouse of Alexandria had stood. It presently serves as a maritime museum.

There are two locations to go if you want to live among the dead. The Mostafa Kamel Cemetery comes first (which is a bit of a hidden gem). It is named for the prominent politician from the 20th century Mostafa Kamel and has four graves that date back more than 2000 years.

After that, if you're still up for it, make your way to Kom el-Shouqafa, which is situated in the town's historic district. It is regarded as one of the Seven Wonders of the Middle Ages and houses a number of Alexandrian tombs, statues, and archaeological artifacts.

Viewing Pompey's Pillar, a huge granite column from the third century AD, will lift your spirits. Explore the area around it to see the nearby sculptures and ruins. The Roman Theatre, which was constructed a century before the Pillar, is the next stop. 800 people could formerly fit inside the spectacular amphitheatre's thirteen tiers, which were constructed entirely of marble.

Your next trip should be Montazah Palace, a significantly more recent structure that was finished in 1892. Although it now has a casino and a five-star hotel, the Montazah Royal Gardens remain the main attraction. You may stroll through these stunning gardens, which even include a beach, for a modest price.

After the garden tour, if you still have time to spend outside, you should visit the Alexandria National Museum. The Alexandria National Museum, which situated in Alexandria's Latin neighborhood, offers a glimpse into ancient archaeology, from Prehistoric items through Islamic-era artifacts.

8. Abu Simbel

The Nubian community of the same name is located about 40 kilometers outside of Sudan and close to Egypt's southern border. The Abu Simbel Temples, also known as the Nubian Monuments, are a UNSECO World Heritage Site that gained national and international attention.

History & Culture

When Rameses II was pharaoh in the 1200s BC, the temple complex was physically chiseled out of the mountainside. To recognize both himself and his wife, Queen Nefertari, for their victory at the Battle of Kadesh, he ordered its built.

The Great Temple and the Small Temple are the two temples there. It took two decades to construct the Great Temple, which is today regarded as one of Egypt's most stunning buildings. Massive 20-meter-tall statues of the Pharaoh, baboons, and sun worshippers are also there. Rameses II statues are easily identified by their twin crown, which symbolizes his rule over both Upper and Lower Egypt.

It's incredible how this temple was built to make the most of the daylight on February 20 and October 20. On certain days, the statues on the back wall of the temple would be illuminated by the sun, with the exception of Ptah, the deity of the underworld, who was always in the shadows. According to legend, the monarch was crowned on October 20 and celebrated his birthday on February 20.

Just one hundred meters separate the Great Temple from the Small Temple, also known as the Temple of Hathor. It was built in honor of both the goddess Hathor and Queen Nefertari. The monarch and queen are depicted in the little over ten-meter-high statues that can be found in front of the temple.

Actually, both temples were moved in the 1960s to keep them from being flooded by Lake Nasser. The entire site was meticulously cut into enormous blocks between 1964 and 1968, weighing up to 30 tons on average, lifted, and then reconstructed 65 meters higher and 200 meters away from the river.

Interior of the Temple of Ramesses II

Attractions & Activities

Everyone visits Abu Simbel to see the two temples' remnants, and you ought to do the same. The Great Temple of Rameses II is larger and more intricate than the Small Temple, yet both are worth the time and money to visit on the inside and exterior. Don't be shocked when you enter the Great Temple and discover that it is situated on an artificial mountainside; this was a necessary evil owing to the relocation, and you might find it amusing.

In general, it is a good idea to research the temples before visiting them, especially if you just have a short amount of time in the afternoon. The impact of these magnificent buildings won't be decreased, and in fact, learning more about them will make you appreciate them even more.

You should be sure not to miss the nightly Sound and Light Show if you are visiting for the evening or intend to spend the night. The winter and summer showtimes are 7 and 8 pm and 8 and 9 pm, respectively. An international audience will like it because they may purchase headphones to listen to the commentary in their own language.

9. The Nile

The Nile, which is well-known as the longest river in the world, is an astonishing 6,853 kilometers long. It passes through eleven nations in Africa and notably travels north. Since it was essentially their primary source of fresh water, it has played a crucial role in the histories of Sudan and Egypt. After going past Cairo, it splits in half, creating the Nile Delta. Both branches, one of which originates in Alexandria, drain directly into the Mediterranean Sea.

History

The Nile, known in Ancient Egypt as "iteru," has been Egypt's primary source of food since the Stone Age. Due to the fact that most of Egypt's major towns are situated along the Nile, planning your travel itinerary while visiting this nation is made much easier.

The Nile provided the Egyptians with drinking water as well as regular overflows that left fertile silt on the ground and promoted easy growth and flourishing of crops. It allowed Egypt to cultivate papyrus, flax, and wheat for trade with a Middle East that was constantly experiencing famine. Egypt was able to stabilize its own wealth while also strengthening its relations with other nations as a result.

Because of how crucial it was to ancient Egypt, the Nile even had an impact on their calendar. The flooding season, the growth season, and the harvest season were modeled after the three Nile cycles.

The Nile also had an impact on religion. The region west of the Nile, where the sun or the god Ra set or died each day before rising the next day on the east, was regarded as the place of death, whereas the eastern side was the place of birth and growth. This explains why the tombs, which include the Giza Pyramids, are situated on the western side.

Sailing on the Nile

Attractions & Activities

Taking a river cruise along the Egyptian Nile is one well-liked way to experience it. These cruises frequently depart from and arrive in Cairo, passing to Giza, Saqqara, Luxor, Edfu, Kom Ombo, and the southernmost city of Aswan before returning to Cairo.

They include stops along the way, frequently overnight ones, so you can fully appreciate the cities and attractions along the Nile. There are several different firms offering these cruises, which range in length from a few days to ten or more.

As an alternative, you may embark on an Aswan-bound felucca cruise. A felucca cruise is a voyage on a traditional wooden sailboat that is propelled only by the wind and the current. It is much more authentic because it moves at a much slower pace than the other cruises.

Typically, felucca cruises are planned individually, allowing you to travel whenever you like. Make sure you bring a sleeping bag because you will dine and sleep aboard the boat. These cruises are ideal for those seeking a more distinctive experience because they are more conventional, more affordable, and more tailored.

Chapter 12:
Best Beaches in Egypt

Many people believe that Egypt is home to pyramids and sand. Here, in Egypt, are some of the nicest beaches in the world that will just astound you. The beaches are like heaven due to their breathtaking scenery, welcoming surroundings, and crystal blue waters. Egypt has another region that is distinct from the part that is well-known to us. You can expect to have all the fun and adventure you can handle at these beaches, which also provide all the different water sports you could possibly want. Choose one of them as your vacation spot and savor the tranquility they offer.

Island of the Pharaoh

This is an amazing diving spot and a place that offers views upto Saudi Arabia and Jordan. There is also a beautiful fortress to visit. You can avail a boat from Taba coast to reach to the Salah El-Din's strategic fortress.

El Gouna

El Gouna is a unique and charming beach that is also a well-known Red Sea destination. A number of islands that are joined by bridges make up this beach. This should unquestionably be on your list because it offers natural beaches, water sports, and bustling marinas. This beach, which has won numerous prizes, including the Golden Green Award, is also one of Egypt's most environmentally friendly vacation spots. Though practically everything allows diving, certain locations are privately held by hotels and resorts. El Gouna's kite-surfing facilities are also well-known, which adds to its allure.

Marsha Allam

Marsha Allam, which is situated on the Red Sea shore, is well-known as a diving enthusiast's vacation spot. Marsha Allam's dive sites are active, living, and teeming with a variety of underwater wildlife action. They may be found between the sea and the mountains. In contrast to other Red Sea resorts, here visitors can engage in activities like snorkeling and glass-bottom boats to experience the wildlife. Astounding on-land adventures are also offered by Marsha Allam. You can explore the Wadi al Gimla and Golden Elba National Parks, as well as numerous unique species and birds, and go on a tour of the area's historic gold and emerald mines. You can enjoy adventure and leisure together at this location.

Soma Bay

Just four square miles make up the secluded peninsula of Soma Bay, which is located on the western shore of the Red Sea. Soma Bay has been ranked as one of the top three kite surfing locations in the world due to its abundance of chances for water sports. Due to its stunning position, which is exclusive and home to numerous upscale resorts, tourists may take advantage of everything the beach has to offer. Visitors can unwind on the beach throughout the day, and some can partake in romantic beachside meals that the resort arranges in the evenings. Take in a beautiful sunset while strolling along the beach. With a diving center and kite safari activities available, the Movepick Resort Soma Bay is a great place to stay with family and friends and enjoy the beach.

Hurghada

Snorkeling, windsurfing, sailing, and deep-sea fishing are popular activities along the Red Sea's great expanses of beach. One of the original Red Sea diving bases is Hurghada. Both public and private beaches are present. The most stunning of these, though, are some that are operated by hotels and resorts. Sahl Hasheesh Bay is located a short distance along the coast and is home to the beaches that the majority of tourists simply like. This is one of the best places in Egypt for a beach vacation because the beaches are 7.5 miles long, have crystal-clear water, and have mountains in the background. Hurghada is a fantastic location from which to visit the stunning beaches on neighboring islands.

Abu Galoum in Dahab

It is renowned for being an amazing diving location, with its beautiful variety of coral reefs, which are magnificent to observe and a great site for hiking as well. Ras Abu Galoum is situated in the natural protected region of Nabq to the north. You may take in the breathtaking views of the nearby coastal mountains from this location.

Ain Al Sokhna

What could be more amazing than really seeing dolphins playing around? That is the beach's best feature. Two hours separate Ain Al Sokhna from the urban jungle. This beach enables visitors to combine a trip to the magnificent Giza pyramids with a tranquil, chilly sunset on the white beach. A tranquil meal can also be had with friends and family at one of the many hotels and resorts close to the beach. Discover different water activities including jet-skiing, kayaking, and wind-surfing.

Ras Shitan

Ras Shitan, another well-known diving location, is found in Northern Nuweiba and is the ideal getaway for anyone seeking peace in a tranquil setting with only the sound of the sea for company. Enjoy a relaxed beach day while admiring the Red Sea's stunning beauty. Every visitor's ideal getaway is a beach camp at this beach, complete with basic bamboo cottages and wooden bungalows. You may enjoy Shitan's diverse marine life by exploring its underwater mountains and caverns. So, if you're looking for a spot to get away from the chaos of your daily life, this well-known resort is a must-visit.

Sharm El-Naga Bay

The northern Safaga is within a few kilometers from Sharm El-Naga Bay. Even though Safaga is a unique Red Sea location well-known for water sports and climatotherapy, it is still underestimated and does not receive as many visitors as it should. The coral reefs are near to the coast, making it possible to see them without having to swim or take a boat a long way offshore. This is the nicest element of this beach. You might see several octopuses here as well. The pristine, crystal-clear waters will leave you in amazement of the vibrant fish, lovely corals, and thriving organisms.

Taba

On the Sinai Peninsula, Taba is one of the most beautiful beaches. This beach boasts some of the most gorgeous views, as well as year-round ideal weather. Enjoy the stunning natural scenery, mountains that are bronze in color, and the Red Sea's brilliant color. Here, on the golden beach, you can ride camels and spend a lovely day drinking hot tea with Bedouins. Only a few amenities are available to you while visiting this lovely beach, including delectable meals and breathtaking vistas.

Marsa Matrouh

Marsa Matrouh is hidden in a coastal cove and shielded from powerful waves by a labyrinth of rocks that serve as a built-in defense. The crown treasure of the Mediterranean Sea is this beach. Take in the serene environment and the sparkling seas, which are distinct from the Mediterranean Sea's choppy and forceful waves. In Marsa Matrouh, you'll experience pure heaven. This beach, which is in the Matrouh Governorate, features stunning seashores that are regarded as some of the best in the world. According to legend, Cleopatra herself took baths in these waters.

Egypt offers some of the world's most stunning beach resorts waiting for you, complete with rugged shorelines, extraordinary marine habitats, and serene, calming waters. Egypt's beaches come in a variety of sizes and shapes, from its picture-perfect beaches to its exceptional weather, which is excellent for any water activity enthusiast. Enjoy your trip to Egypt, and don't forget to soak in the breathtaking natural scenery the country has to offer in addition to your recollections of the pyramids and other historic structures.

how to get in touch with the local culture

Egypt is a country with a rich history and culture that spans thousands of years. From the ancient pyramids to the bustling markets of Cairo, there is so much to see and experience in this fascinating country. To truly immerse yourself in the local culture, here are some tips to keep in mind:

Try local food: Egyptian cuisine is delicious and varied, with dishes that reflect the country's diverse history and geography. Be sure to try local specialties like ful medames (fava beans), koshari (a mix of rice, lentils, and pasta), and molokhia (a soup made with jute leaves).

Visit local markets: Markets are a great place to experience everyday life in Egypt and interact with locals. You'll find everything from fresh produce to handmade crafts, and it's a great opportunity to practice your bargaining skills.

Learn about local customs and traditions: Egyptians have a rich and diverse culture with many customs and traditions that vary by region. Some customs to be aware of include the importance of hospitality, respect for elders, and modest dress. It's also a good idea to learn about local religious practices and holidays, as these can impact daily life in Egypt.

Engage with locals: One of the best ways to learn about local customs and traditions is by engaging with locals. This can be as simple as striking up a conversation with a shopkeeper or asking for recommendations from your hotel staff. Egyptians are generally friendly and welcoming, and many will be happy to share their culture with you.

Attend local events and festivals: Egypt has a rich calendar of events and festivals that celebrate its history and culture. Attending these events is a great way to learn more about the country and its people, and to experience local traditions first-hand.

By following these tips, you'll be able to experience the rich culture of Egypt and make lasting memories on your trip.

Chapter 13: Local Dishes You Must Try in Egypt

Egypt is arguably one of the few destinations that everyone who travels wants to visit. The traditional gastronomy of Egypt is the country's other well-known attraction, in addition to the pyramids and the Red Sea. Egypt's cuisine incorporates all of the old traditions, and as a result, this civilisation has left its stamp on the world through its traditional foods. They get together and rejoice with their friends and families during their significant events and festivals while enjoying excellent meals with a traditional flavor.

Fattah

The Egyptian version of Fattah, which is well-known throughout the Middle East, is frequently connected with festivals and celebrations, such as weddings and the birth of a new child. Since the beginning of time, this custom has existed. Particularly at Eid-al-Adha, the sacrifice-filled feast that signals the end of

Ramadan fasting, it is served. Crispy bread, rice, pork, and tomato or garlic sauce are all ingredients in this dish. Lamb is utilized on exceptional occasions instead of beef, which is the norm. It is frequently consumed the Lebanese manner, with chicken from the rotisserie, Tamiya, and. Even though this is well-known for being calorific, you won't be dissatisfied.

Kushari

The most affordable and distinctively Egyptian food is called Kushari, which is also spelled Koshary. Kushari, which is served in all Egyptian eateries, has developed into something of a cult phenomenon. This is also regarded as Egypt's national dish. Rice, spaghetti, round macaroni, and black lentils are expertly combined in this mouthwatering dish, which is finished with a rich tomato sauce, garlic, vinegar, and chili. Then, whole chickpeas and crispy fried onions are added as garnishes to this real jumble of ingredients. This dish may sound weird, yet it has an amazing fusion of tastes and textures that both residents and visitors find to be quite addicting. In addition, as it is made entirely of vegetable oil and is vegetarian in every way, everyone is invited to try this well-known Egyptian meal.

Sahlab

This decadent treat's rich flavor and thickness come from the heated milk that is combined with genuine orchid root powder. This powder and other components like vanilla, sugar, and cinnamon can be found as quick sachets that can be used to make this recipe. You can customize it according to your tastes and preferences and add any toppings you desire. To enhance the flavor, add additional coconut, crumbled pistachios, and raisins.

Mulukhiya

This Egyptian dish is called after a plant of the same name and is variously written mulukhiya, molokiya, and moroheiya. In English, mulukhiya is essentially jute. The secret of this recipe is that the very green and leafy vegetable is finely diced and cooked with garlic, lemon juice, and spices until it resembles a thick stew. It is nearly never eaten raw. Although it has a slimy texture, the flavor is really intense. You'll become engrossed in its lovely perfume. You can serve mulukhiya by itself over rice, bread, or even with pieces of meat.

Sayadeya

This one is for those who enjoy seafood. A coastal delicacy called sayadeya is best enjoyed in beach towns like Alexandria, Suez, and Port Said. The dish calls for lightly fried fresh white fish that has been marinated in lemon juice and seasonings. Afterward, the fish is placed over the rice and baked in an earthenware pot with a rich tomato and onion sauce on top. It is preferable to eat this delicious meal, especially during festivals, when the fish is at its softest and will melt at the touch of a fork. Sayadeya is presented by adding fried onions or flakes chili to the dish.

Hamam Mahshi

Even though young pigeon or squab is not a common meat in Western culture, it is a well-known delicacy in Egypt. Due to its reputation as a delicacy and the fact that it is also thought to be aphrodisiac, hamam mahshi is a preferred choice for weddings. Dark meat, which has a distinct flavor of its own, is served in this meal. A entire squab that has been stuffed with freekeh, finely chopped onions, giblets, and spices is used to make this dish. Following that, the chicken is cooked over a wood fire or in a pit roast until its skin is golden brown and delectably crispy.

Fuul Medames

This is one of the most popular meals in Egypt and a staple breakfast item. The recipe takes a lot of time to create and is made with fava beans, oil, and lemon juice. Depending on your preferences, you may also add garlic or onion. In addition to butter, spicy oil, olive oil, tomato sauce to add tang, pepper, pastrami, parsley, sausage, and boiled or even fried eggs, there are many other ways to prepare fuul medames. This dish is more fascinating to eat because it is thought that the recipe came from ancient Egypt.

Hawawshi

This dish is typically prepared in Egypt using pita, meat, onions, pepper, parsley, and occasionally chillies as seasonings. It is offered as a side dish in restaurants and as a well-liked option for grab-and-go street cuisine. In a traditional wood oven, it is essentially a sandwich with ham or ground beef that has been completely encased in aish baladi bread. Try making hawawshi with crushed red chile for an additional kick.

1Umm Ali

This dish is said to have originated in the third century, when Sultan Ezz El Din Aybak's wife prepared it for a victory celebration and served it to the local populace. This warming delicacy is topped with a mixture of raisins and almonds, chunks of coconut, and is served hot. It combines the sweet flavors of bread, milk, and sugar. If you want to make it even more delectable, you may also add dry fruits.

Konafa

This incredibly popular treat, which is composed with shredded Konafa pieces and is filled with thick cream or cheese before being baked and served with syrup, is regarded as the queen of Egyptian sweets. Two layers of extremely thin semolina flour noodles make up the original version of this meal, which is typically given during Ramadan to keep people satisfied throughout the fasting hours. The noodles can also be swapped out for thin strips of filo pastry or sun-dried wheat, and the filling can range from custard to mixed nuts. You may find this Konafa at several bakeries and restaurants in their updated form, which incorporates mango, chocolate, and even avocado.

Falafel

This classic Egyptian meal, also known as Ta'meya, is often eaten as a typical breakfast and is accompanied by cheese, effs, and pita bread. In order to make the Ta'meya or Falafel, fava beans are crushed and combined with other ingredients. It frequently comes with salad and tahini as well. The vegans will also love this dish. Also a very well-liked street snack. They are vegan, reasonably priced, and absolutely wonderful. It's a must try while visiting Egypt because it's bursting with distinct and fresh flavor.

Egyptian food has a rich history and will ensure that you leave this nation with the taste and flavors so you can always remember the essence of this lovely culture. Their cuisine primarily relies on the abundant harvest of fruits and vegetables that occurs annually in the fertile Nile Delta. Egyptian cuisine offers a broad variety of alternatives, from delectable dishes of meat to delectable dishes of vegetables, and you shouldn't miss their well-known seafood and desserts. Enjoy the sweet flavor of Egypt's cuisine together with the unusual spices.

Chapter 14:
Tips On Currency Exchange

When visiting Egypt, keep in mind the following advice on currency exchange and where to do it:

1. **Currency:** The Egyptian pound is the official currency in Egypt (EGP). It is advised to keep some local money on hand for small transactions and gratuities.

2. **Exchange Rates:** Exchange rates fluctuate depending on where and how currency is exchanged. Before your travel, it's crucial to investigate the most competitive exchange rates.

3. **Exchange at the airport:** There are currency exchange counters at the airport in Egypt. These might be practical, but they might also have greater fees and worse exchange rates than other choices.

4. **Exchange at Banks:** Egypt's banks provide currency exchange services, and they are typically a dependable and secure option. It's best to check with your bank ahead of time because some banks might charge costs for currency exchange.

5. **Exchange at exchange offices**: In Egypt, there are also exchange offices, commonly known as exchange bureaus or forex bureaus. Compared to banks or airport exchange desks, these offices often provide competitive exchange rates and cheaper fees. However, it's

crucial to confirm that the exchange office is reliable and authorized.

6. **Use ATMs:** In general, ATMs are a simple and secure means to withdraw local cash and are commonly distributed in Egypt. However, it's best to check with your bank beforehand as some ATMs could charge fees for overseas withdrawals.

7. **Credit cards:** In Egypt, especially in tourist locations, major credit cards like Visa and Mastercard are commonly accepted. It's crucial to let your bank know about your vacation intentions and to confirm whether there are any international transaction costs.

In general, it's preferable to explore available possibilities for currency conversion in advance and compare prices and costs. When traveling in Egypt, it's also crucial to keep your belongings secure, including your cash and critical papers.

Egypt Maps

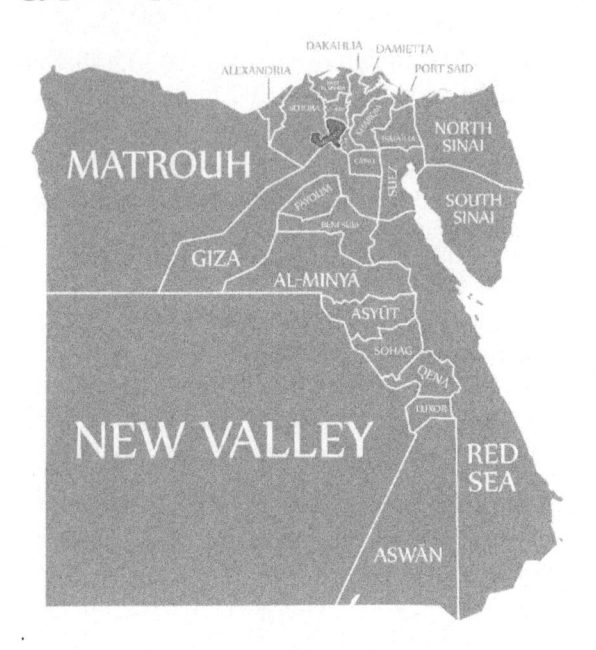

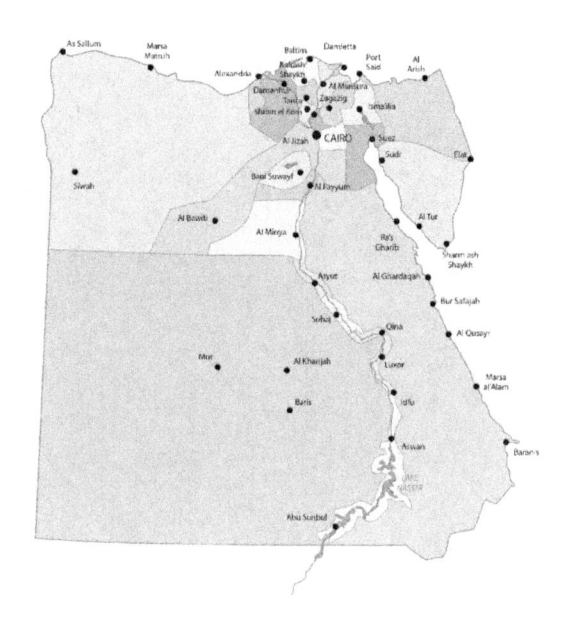

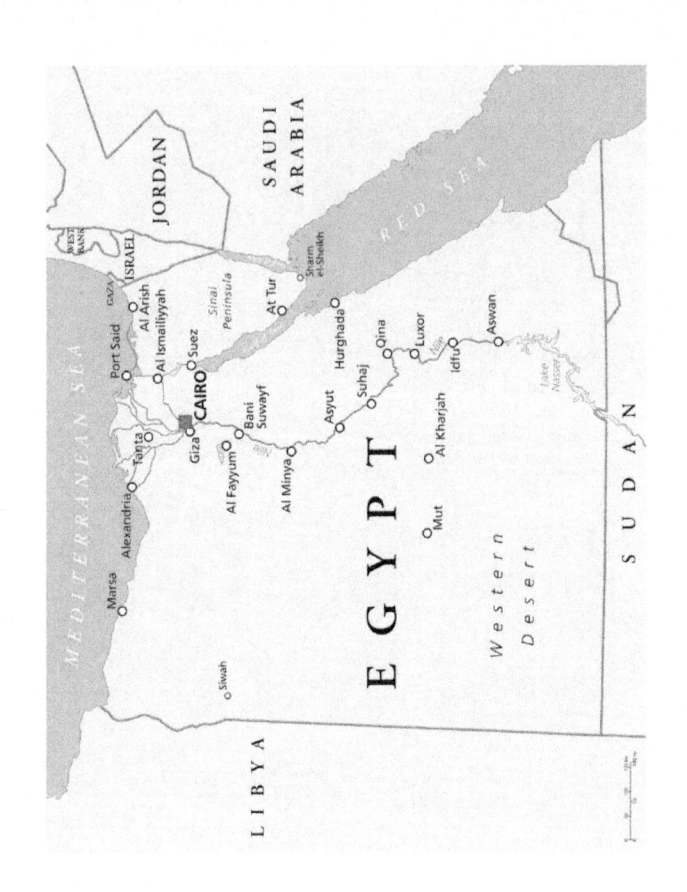

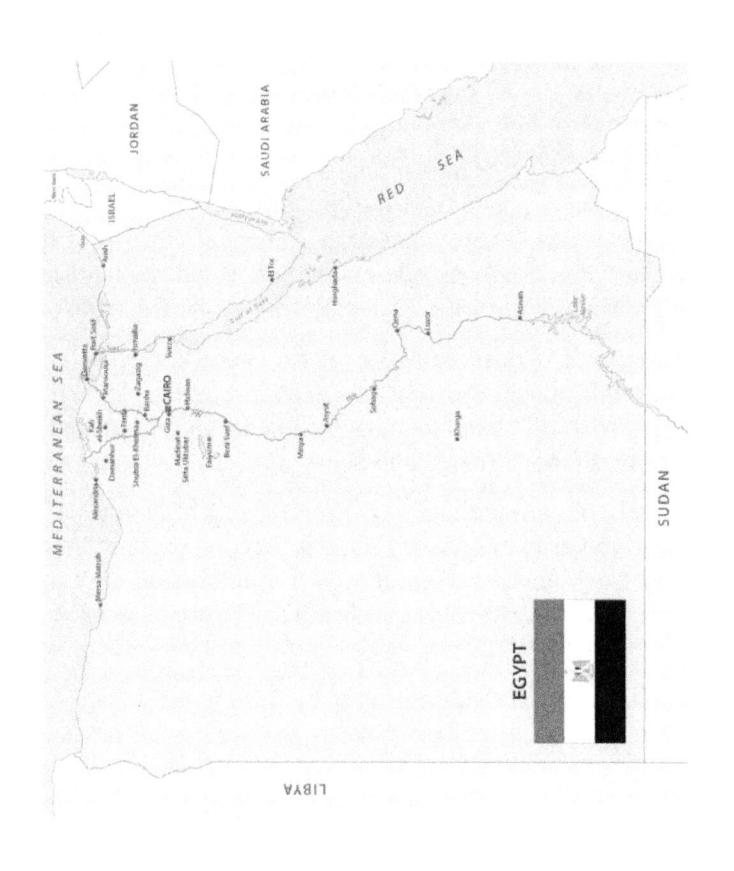

Conclusion

Traveling in 2023 doesn't have to be boring. There are several new travel destinations and experiences that you can enjoy this year or in the near future with plenty of adventure and excitement. This travel guide will provide you with some helpful tips for the trip.

This book is designed to provide useful information that will make your trip to Egypt in 2023 a pleasant one. With all the information and tips you learned, prepare for the trip of a lifetime.

This book will guide you through everything you will need to know in order to make the trip a success. You will learn about places, things to do and see, how to dress and how to get around, and the best practices for traveling in 2023.

Thank you for reading this book. It is your chance to meet the people of Egypt, and to find new experiences. Enjoy your time there!